PAUL SARKISIAN

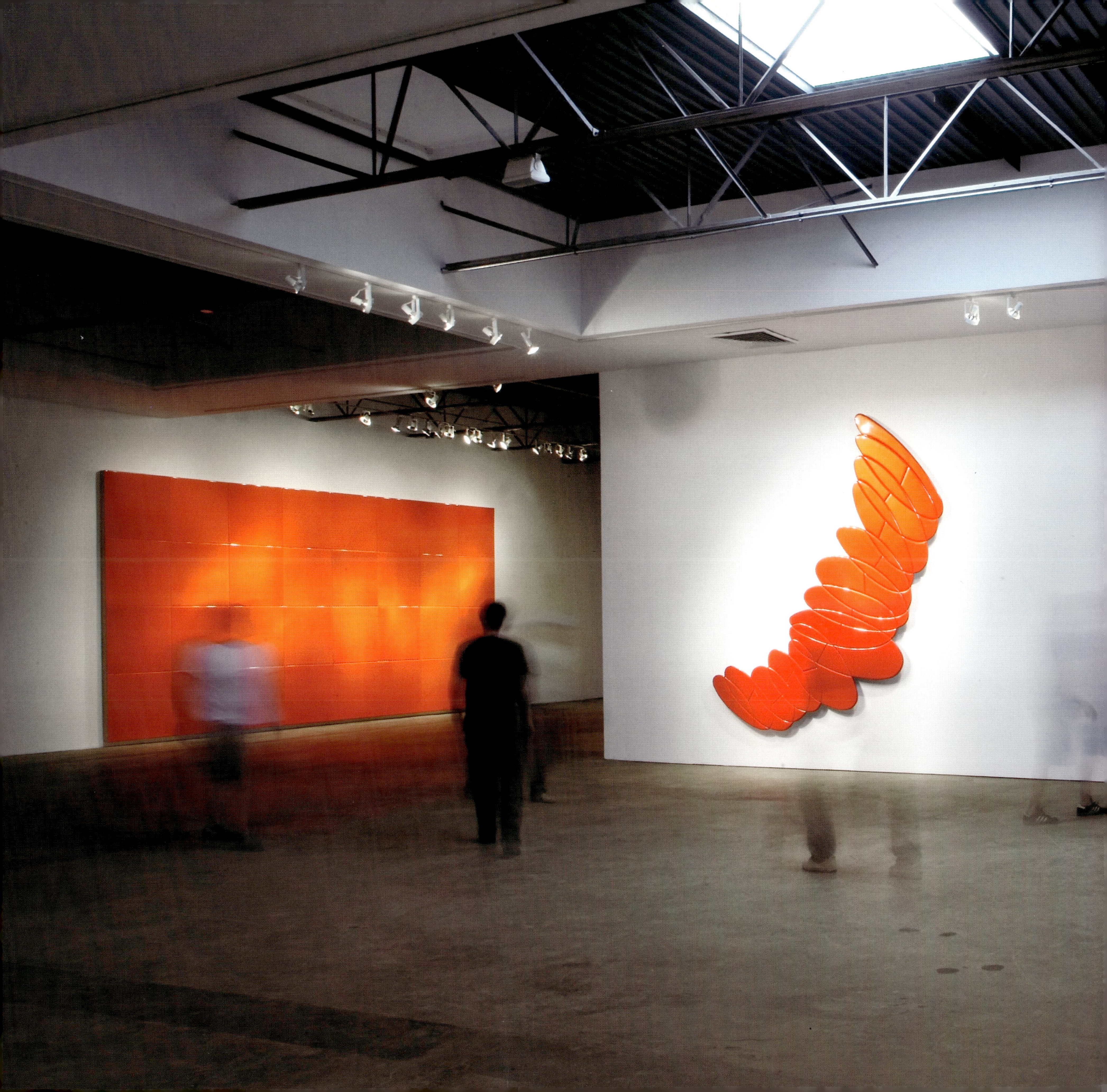

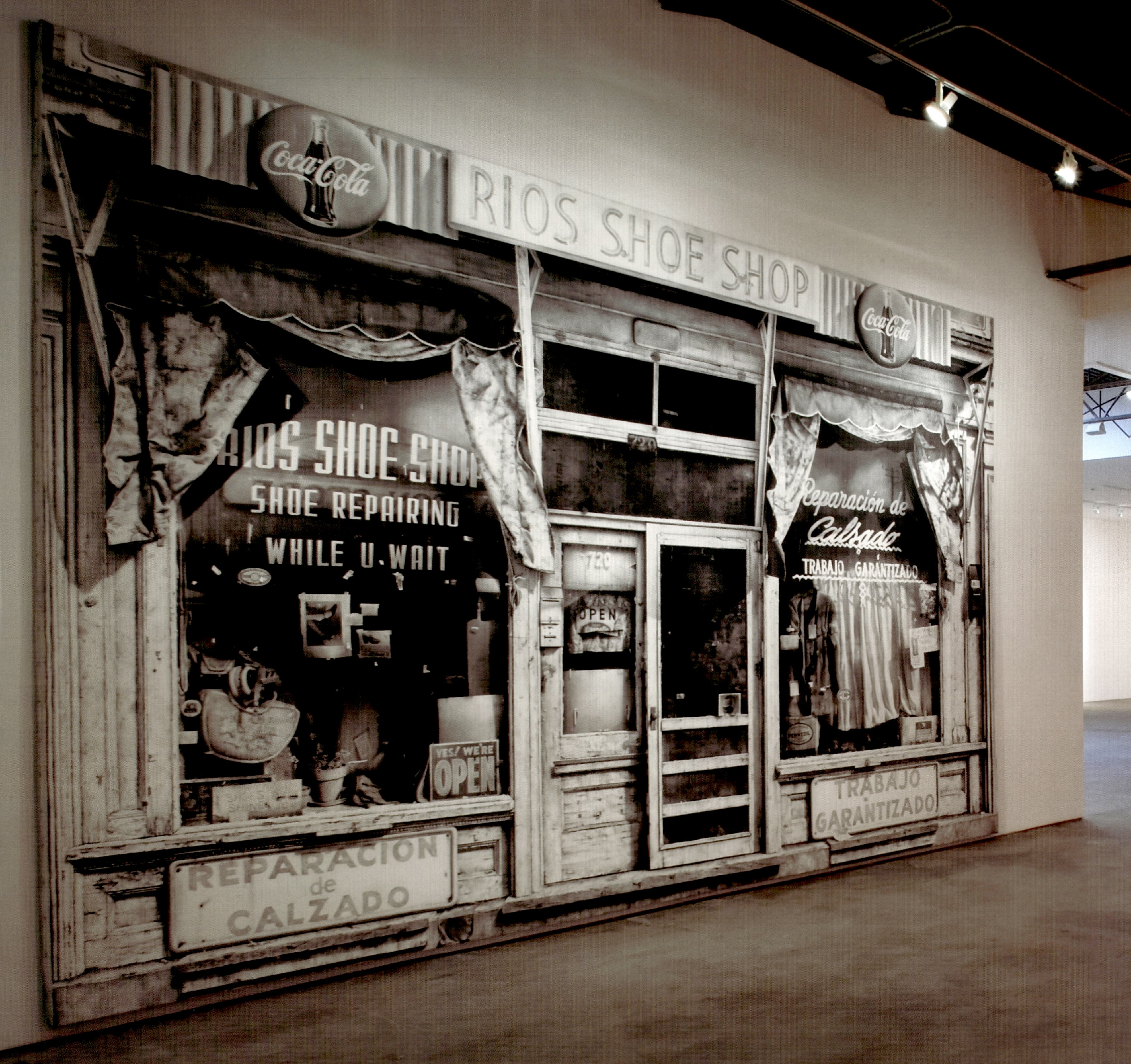
Coca-Cola
RIOS SHOE SHOP
Coca-Cola
RIOS SHOE SHOP
SHOE REPAIRING
WHILE U. WAIT
720
Reparación de
Calzado
TRABAJO GARANTIZADO
720
OPEN
YES! WE'RE
OPEN
TRABAJO
GARANTIZADO
REPARACION
de
CALZADO

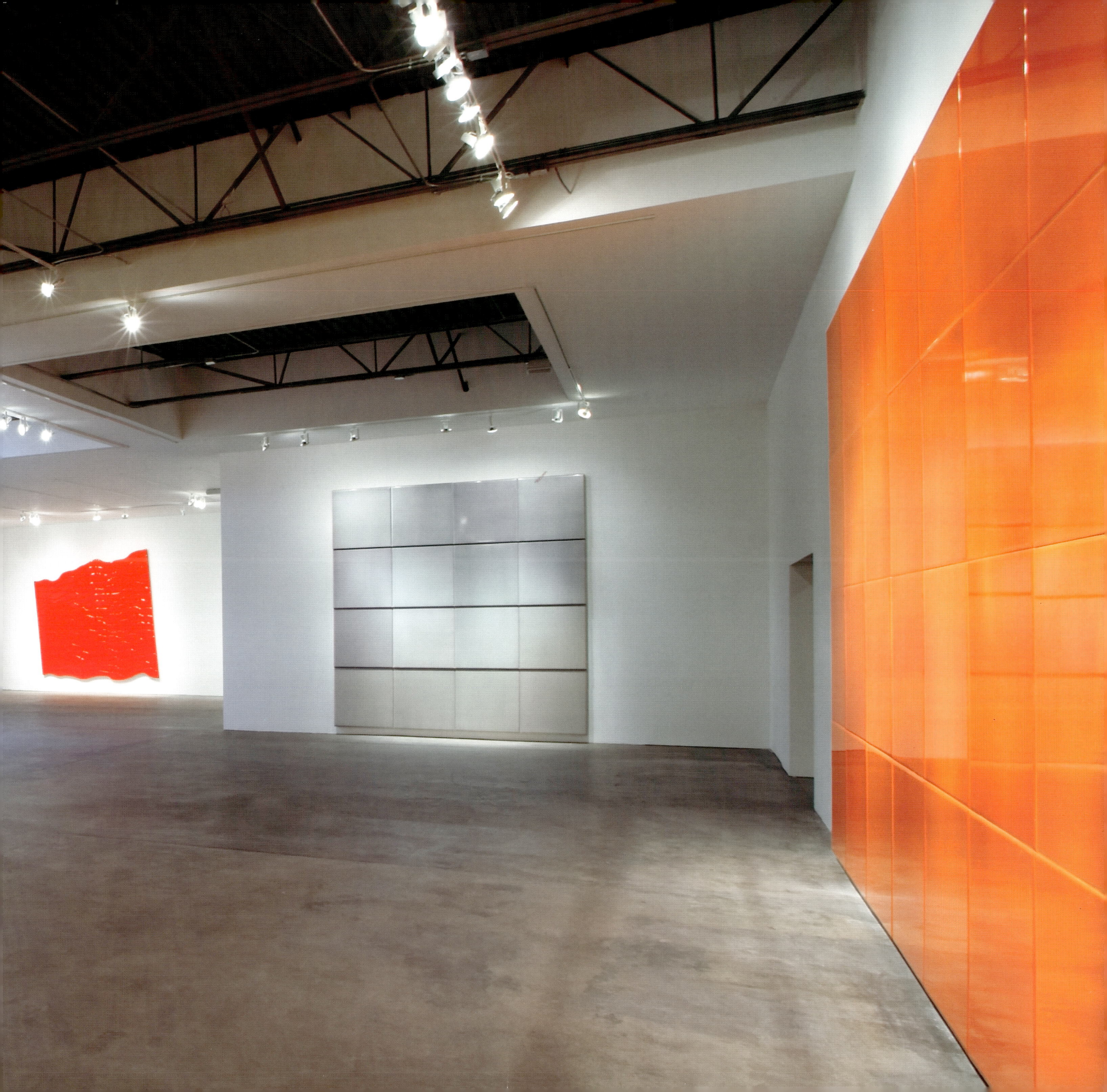

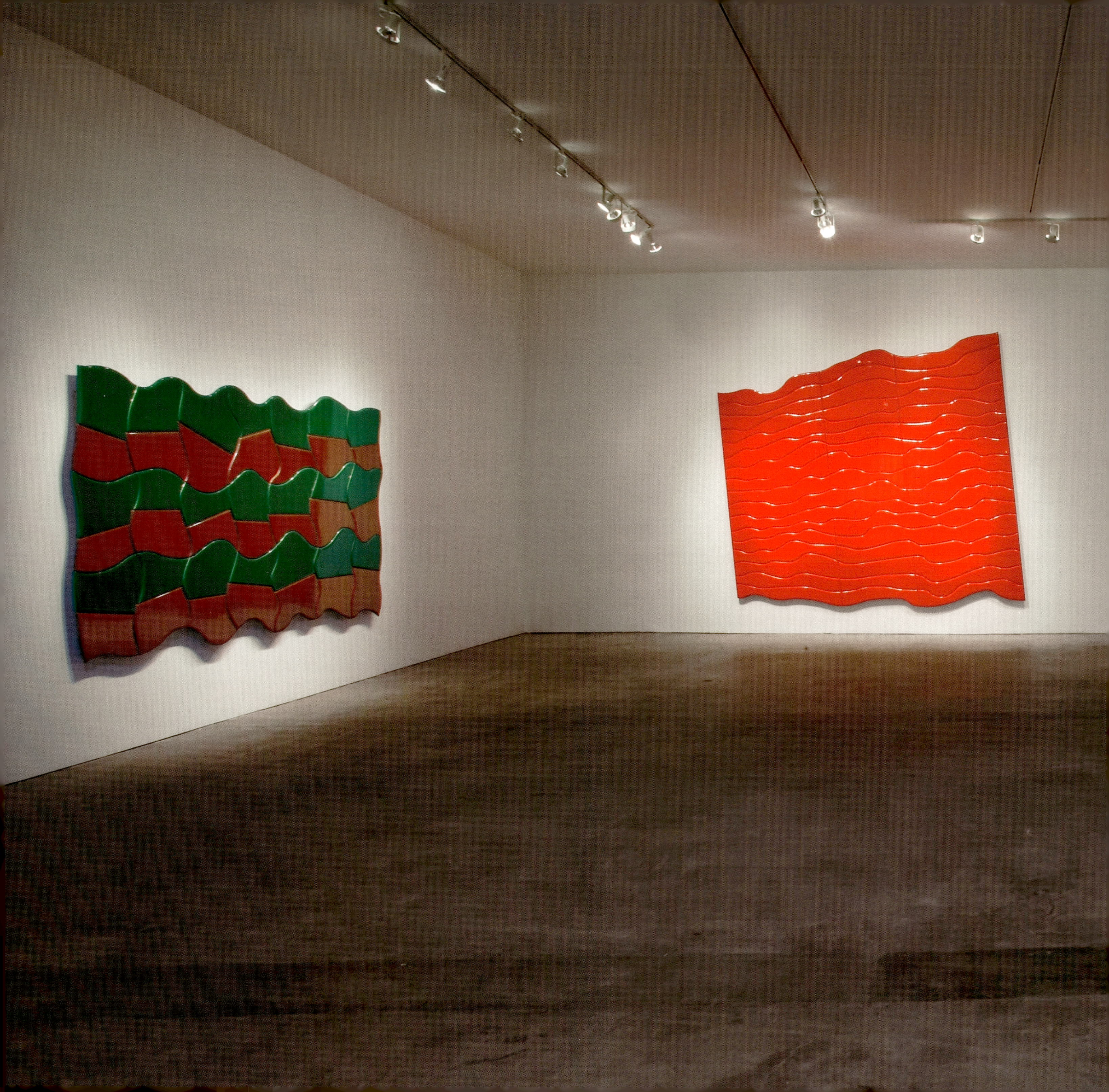

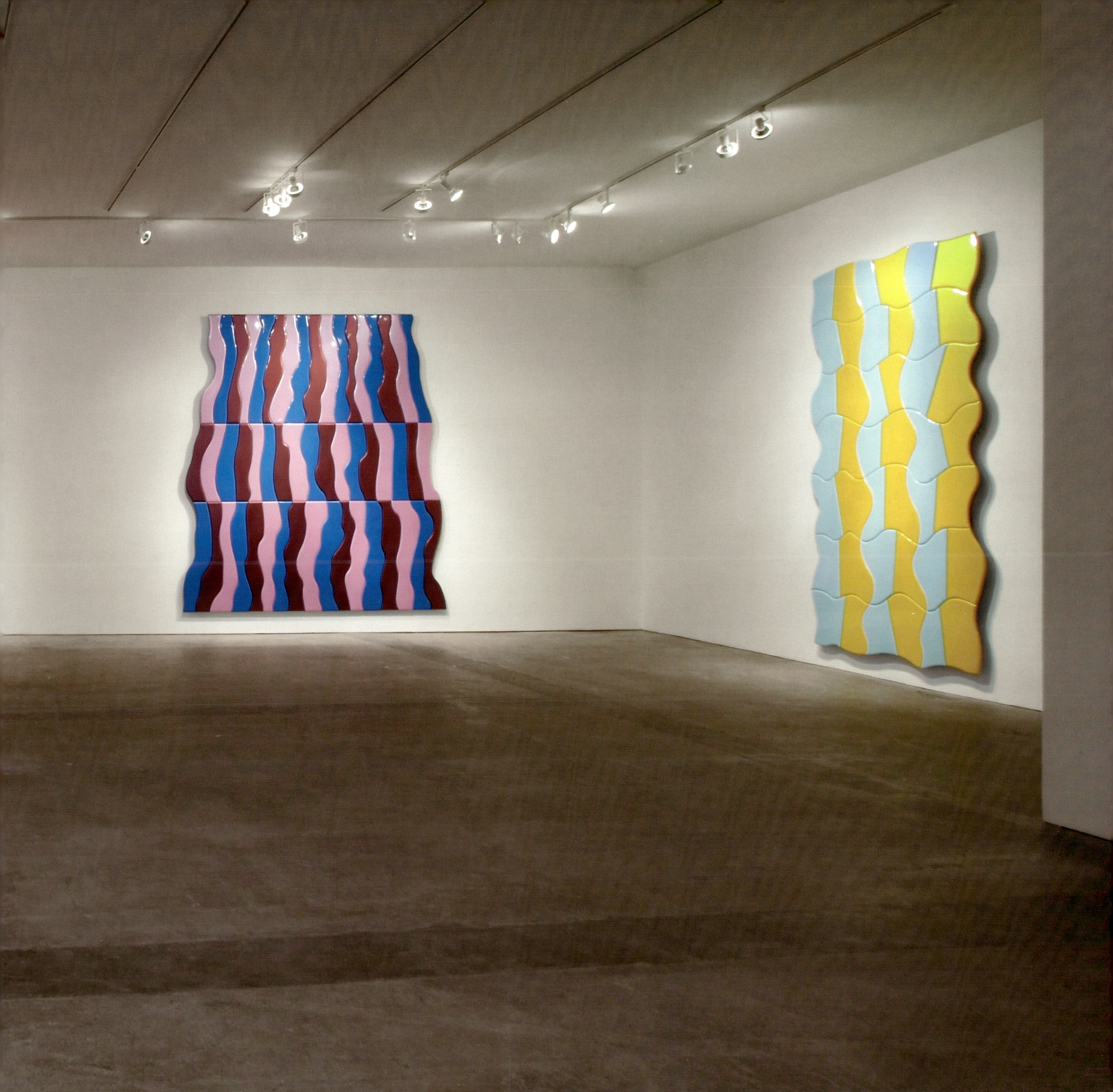

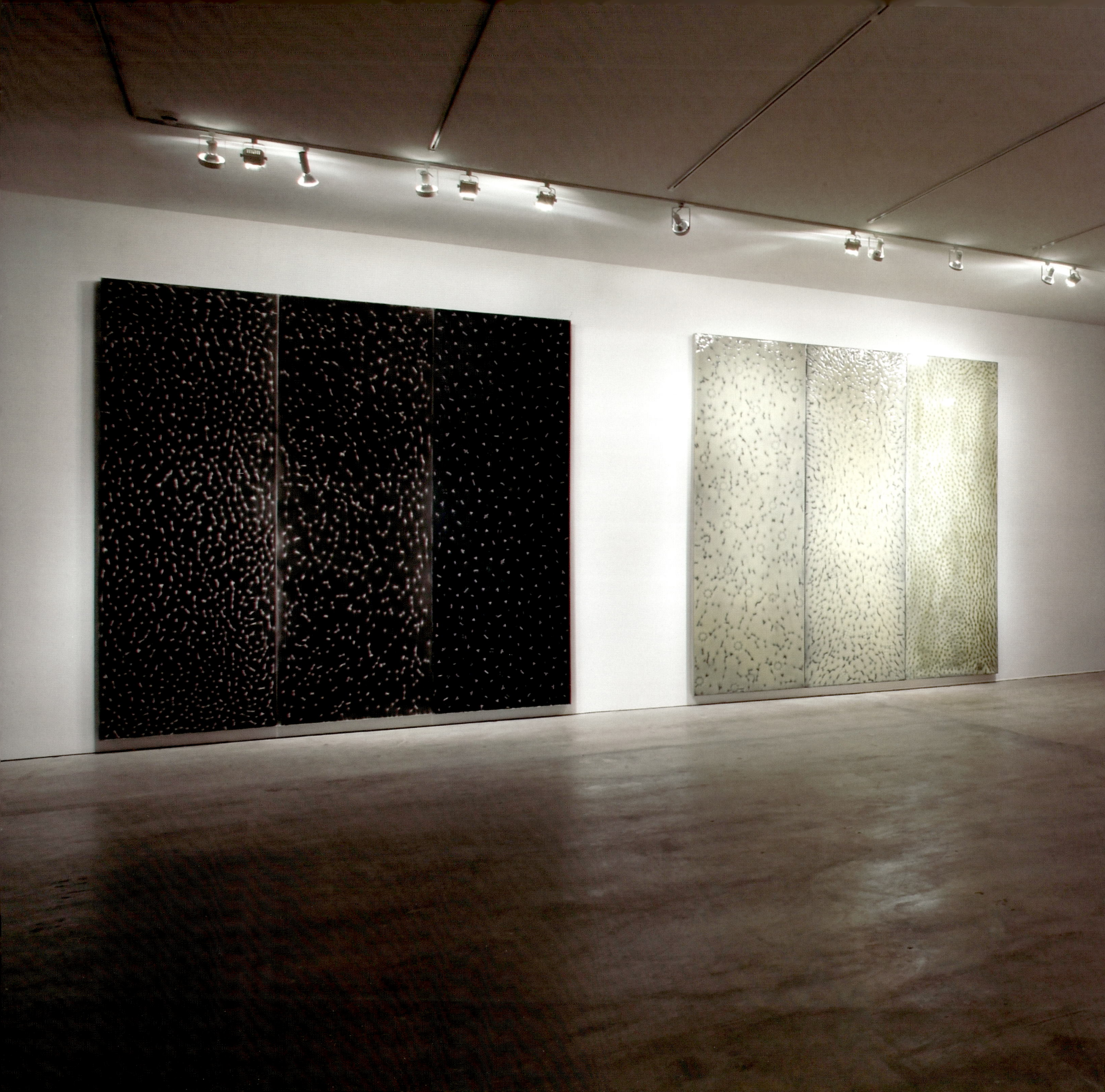

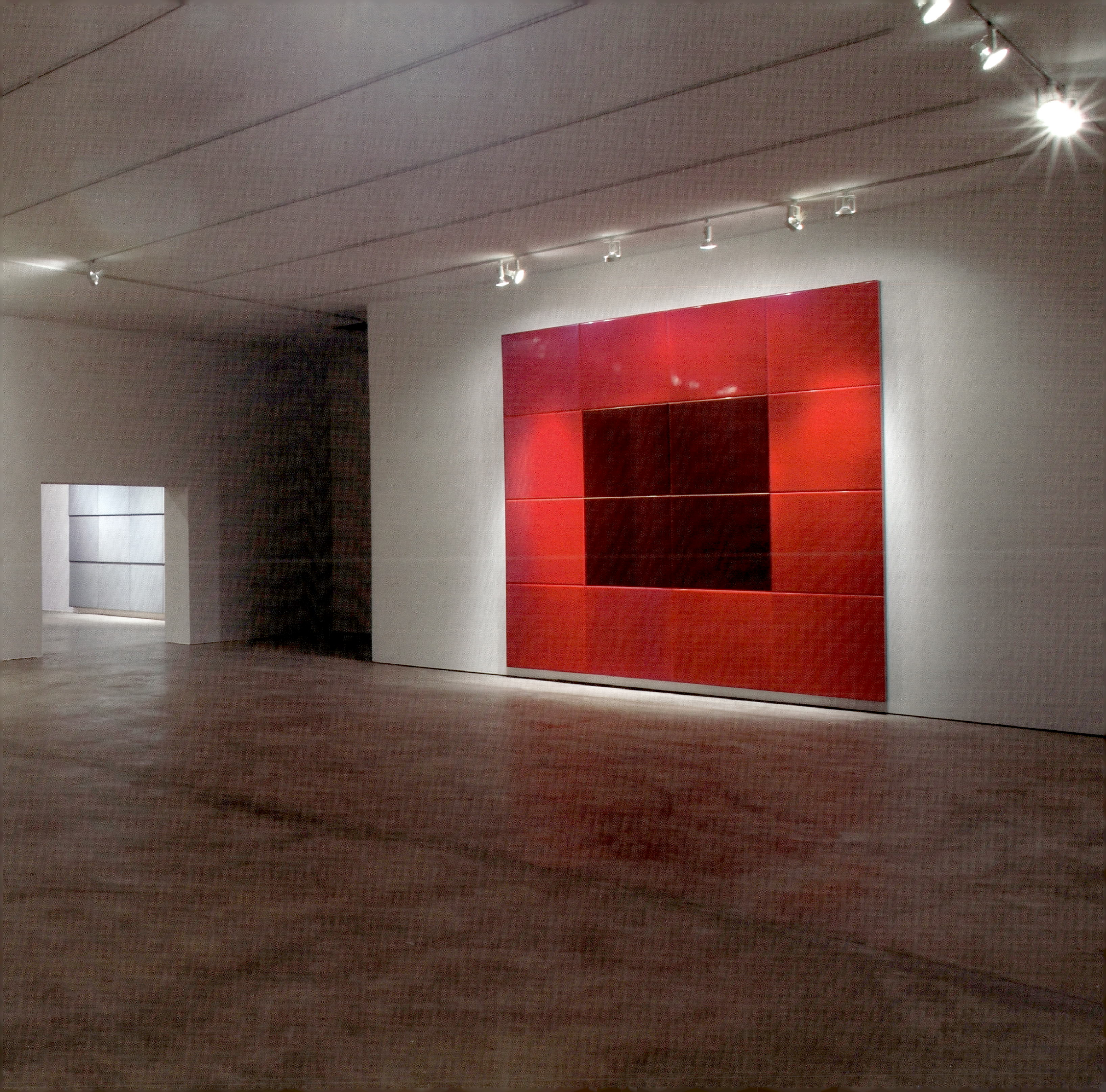

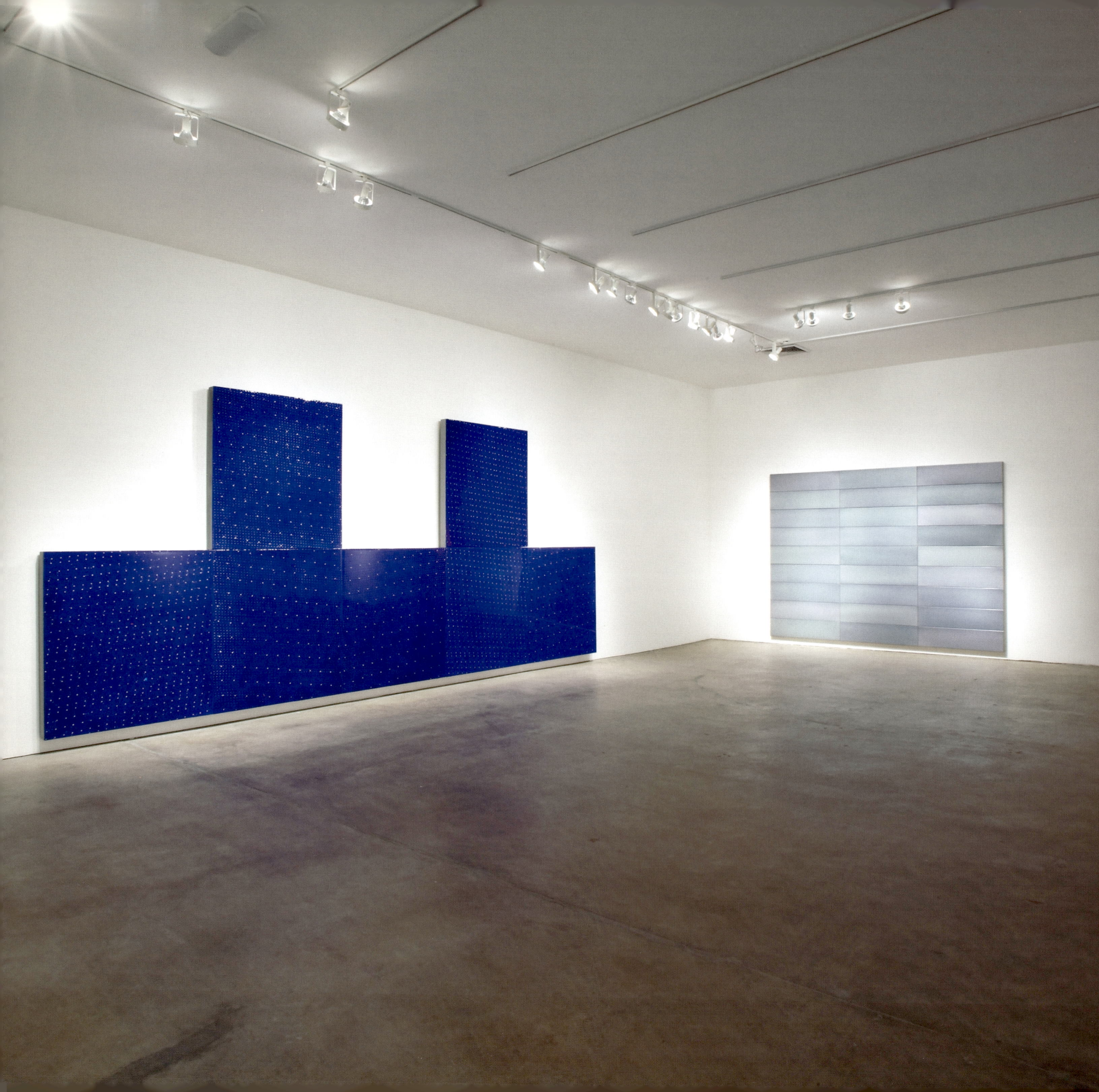

PAUL SARKISIAN

SITE Santa Fe

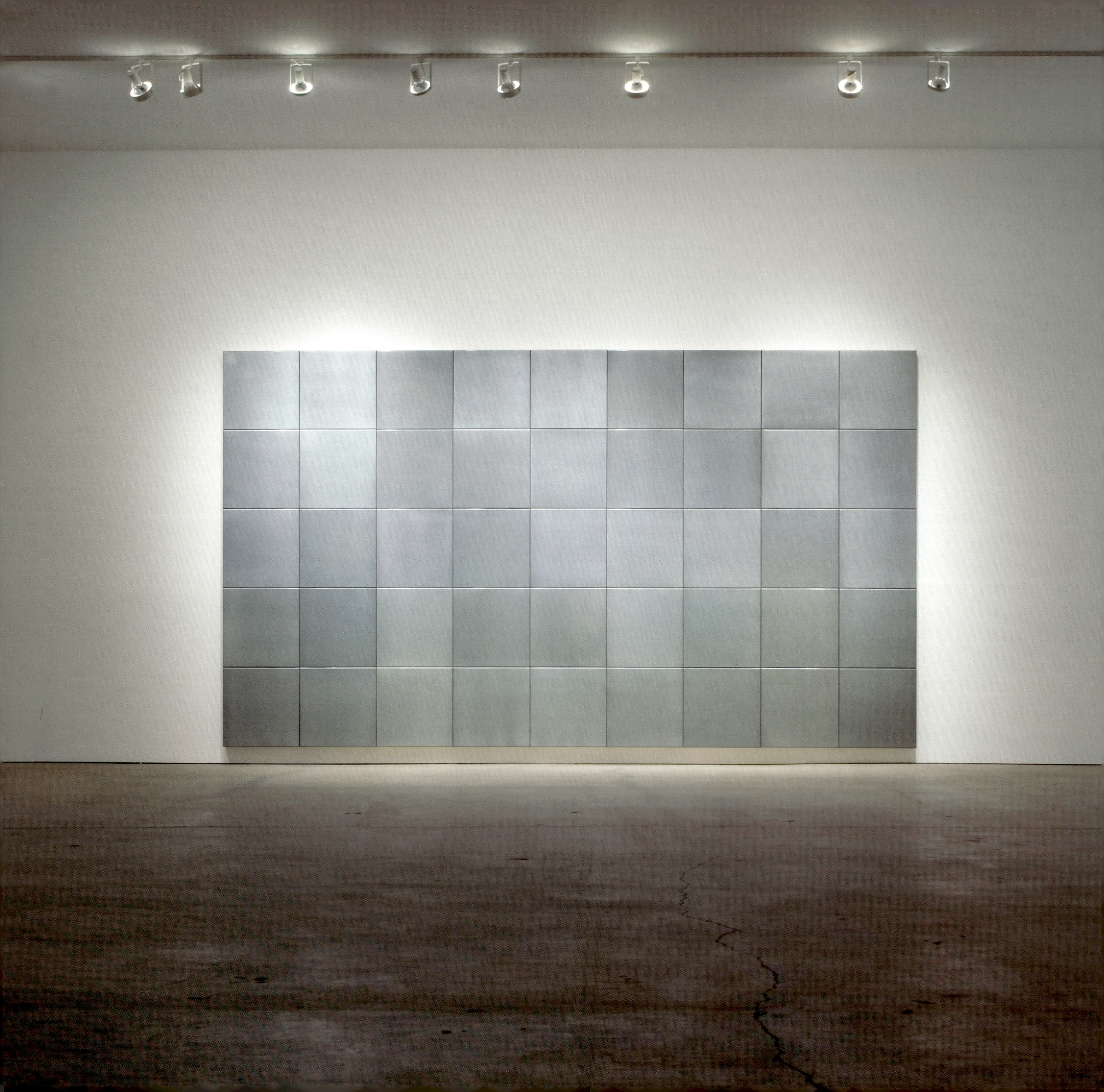

CONTENTS

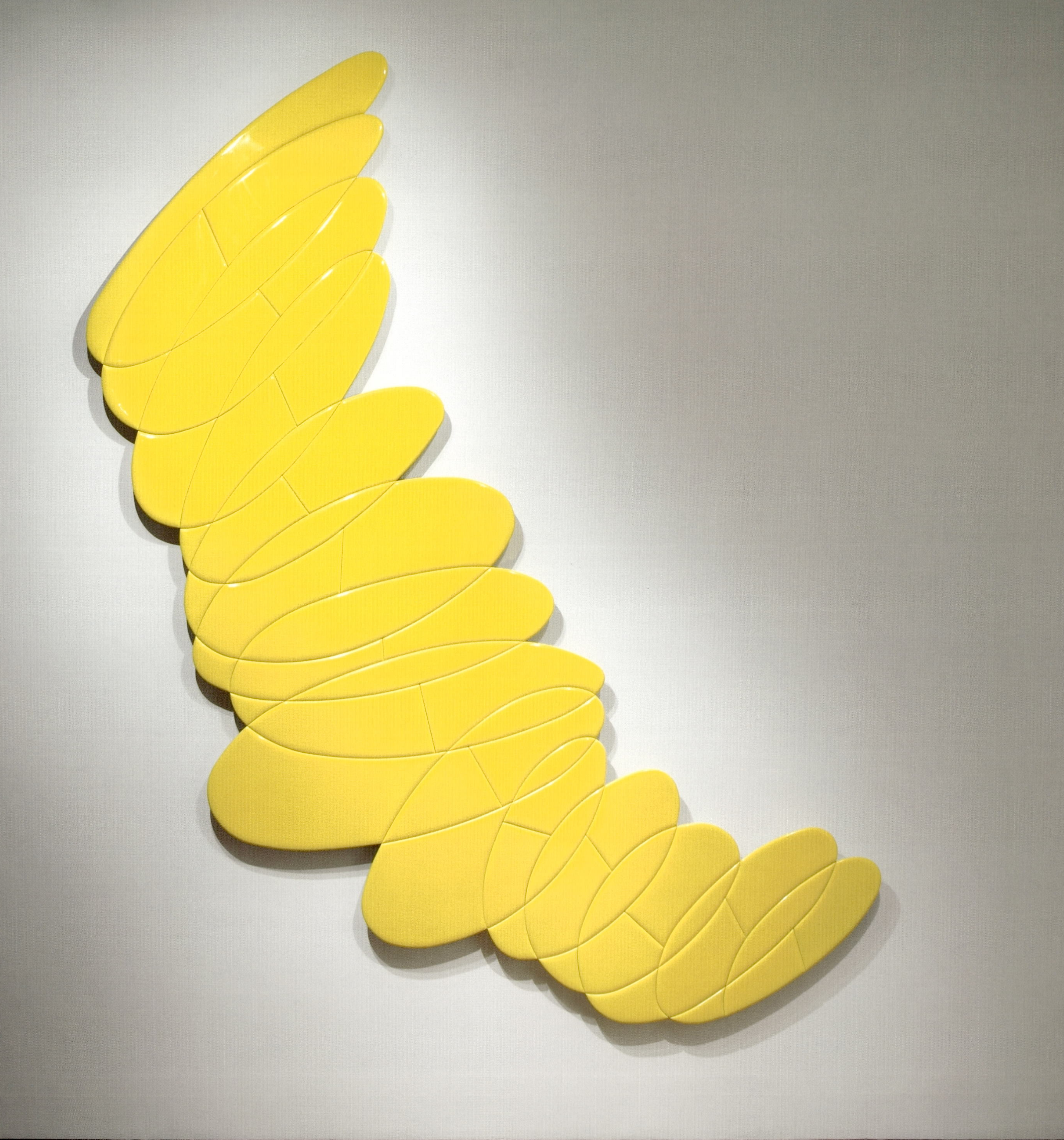

INTRODUCTION

SINCE THE 1950s, PAUL SARKISIAN'S DEEP COMMITMENT to the art and language of painting has been reflected in his extraordinarily innovative and stylistically diverse oeuvre that alludes to artists and trends such as the Finish Fetish group, Abstract Expressionism, and Color Field painting, as well as Conceptual and Pop art. Beginning with his days as a young artist in Los Angeles, his affiliations amongst a wide circle of contemporaries included John Altoon, John Baldessari, Robert Irwin, and Ed Ruscha, along with Bay Area figuration painter Richard Diebenkorn and Beat movement artists Ed Kienholz and George Herms. Sarkisian's idiosyncratic aesthetic and technical virtuosity can be evidenced from the onset of his long and industrious career marked by stylistically extreme and thematic shifts, and through his unending experimentations with unconventional mediums. For example, Sarkisian's early abstract-expressionist paintings (1953–58)—composed of blunted and organic shapes, accentuated by bright gestural strokes of color against muted backgrounds—incorporate materials such as gesso, tar, and mud.

In the ensuing decades—from the early 1960s through the mid-1980s—the artist made a radical departure from nonrepresentational work to depictions of figurative subject matter that ascribe to elements of Surrealism, Illusionism, Photorealism, and even religious iconography. This body of work ultimately led to his critically acclaimed series of monumentally scaled, hyperrealistic paintings of building and storefront façades that were included in *Documenta V* held in Kassel, Germany. Though flatly rendered, their immediacy and life-size depictions, filled with verisimilar details, create visual environments that diminish the distinctions between painting, sculpture, and architecture.

Eventually, Sarkisian's protean course prompted him to extract various elements derived from these façades, which he then integrated as trompe-l'oeil motifs into abstract-geometric compositions reminiscent of the painted collages of Georges Braque. (Between 1973 and 1985, Sarkisian produced more than 200 of these works primarily in acrylic on linen.) Referring back to both his abstract and realist compositions, these striking juxtapositions blur the boundaries between illusion and reality as they lay out the conceptual passages for the artist's subsequent work.

opposite: *Untitled (left leaning yellow51)*, 2005, polyurethane on wood, 14' × 7' 5"
page 11: *Untitled (silver45)*, 2004, polyurethane on wood, 9' 3" × 16' 8"

In the late 1980s, Sarkisian's work effortlessly segued into new structural, spatial, and chromatic arenas triggered by his experimentation with a large-format printing press. During that time, the artist produced numerous prints using a wet-transfer process on which he collaged rag paper. The rich tactility achieved through fusions of color and the thick clusterings of paper over their surfaces makes these prints the evident precursors to the artist's recent work.

While investigating the expressive possibilities of new industrial mediums, Sarkisian began using polymer resin mixed with pigment, synthetic fabrics, and foam densely layered over various surfaces to achieve an array of illusionistic textures and translucent effects. These processes produced an entirely new body of abstract work composed of expansive, shimmering planes of fluctuating and reflected silvery, iridescent, and multicolored tonalities. Evincing both the physical and the conceptual, they serve as vehicles for the projection and transmutation of light beyond their surfaces. These pieces move color into form; space into meditative spheres; and the viewer into perceptual domains punctuated by deep inhalations of color.

Using the latest in cutting-edge technology, Sarkisian's newest paintings are shaped and made with resin and automotive enamel. Often multipaneled, several of these works are rendered in brilliant monochromatic yellows and cadmium reds. Others, striped with wide undulating ribbons of contrasting or complementary colors reminiscent of biomorphic Arp-like forms, feature irregular edges that optically dematerialize on the walls.

Extending the practices of painting while pushing the parameters of materiality, this recent body of work—and the subject of his exhibition—is further testimony to Sarkisian's brilliant innovations in his ongoing and complex pursuits of color and surface.

—LOUIS GRACHOS

Louis Grachos, who served as guest curator for this exhibition, is currently the director of the Albright-Knox Art Gallery in Buffalo, New York.

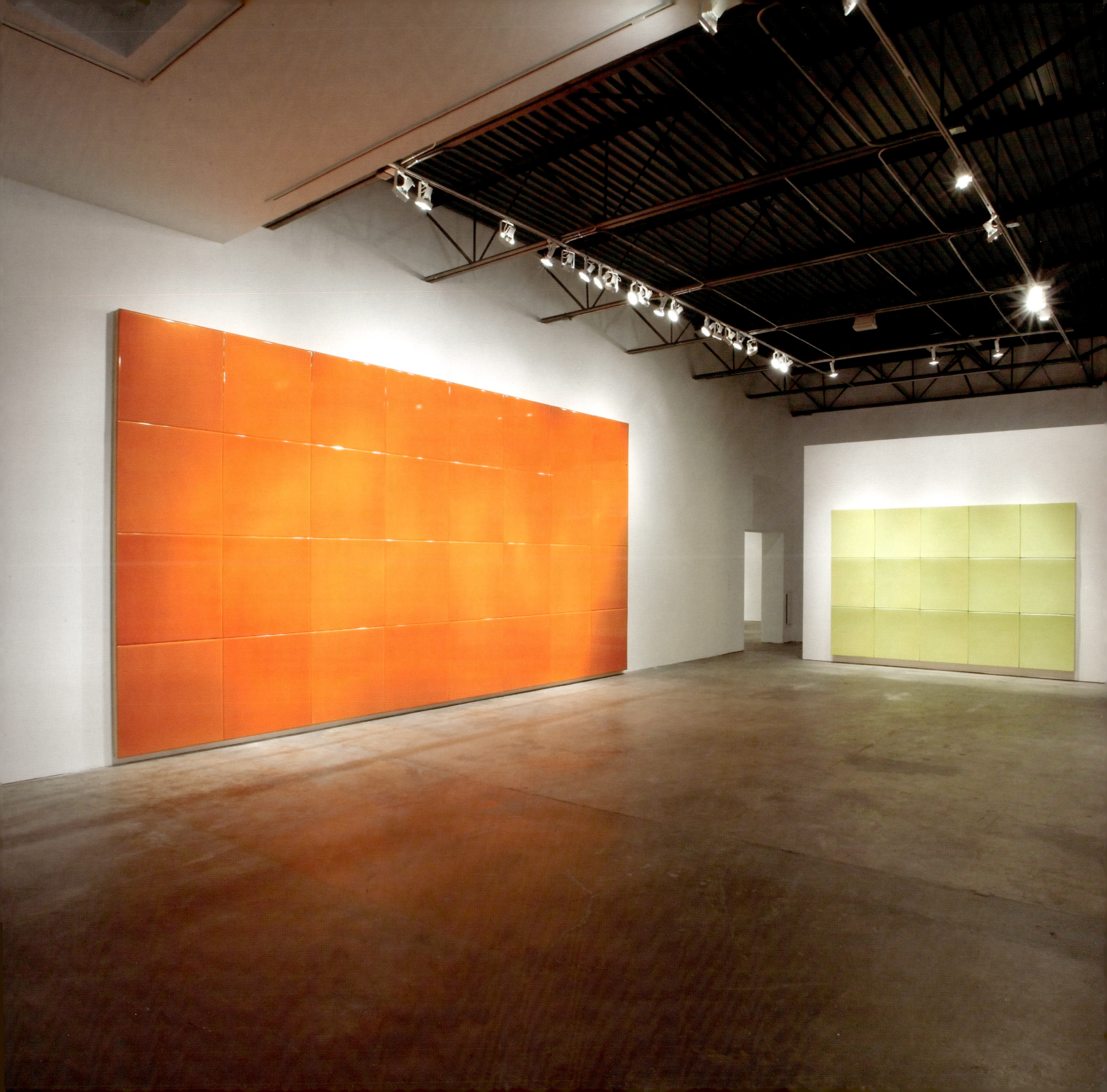

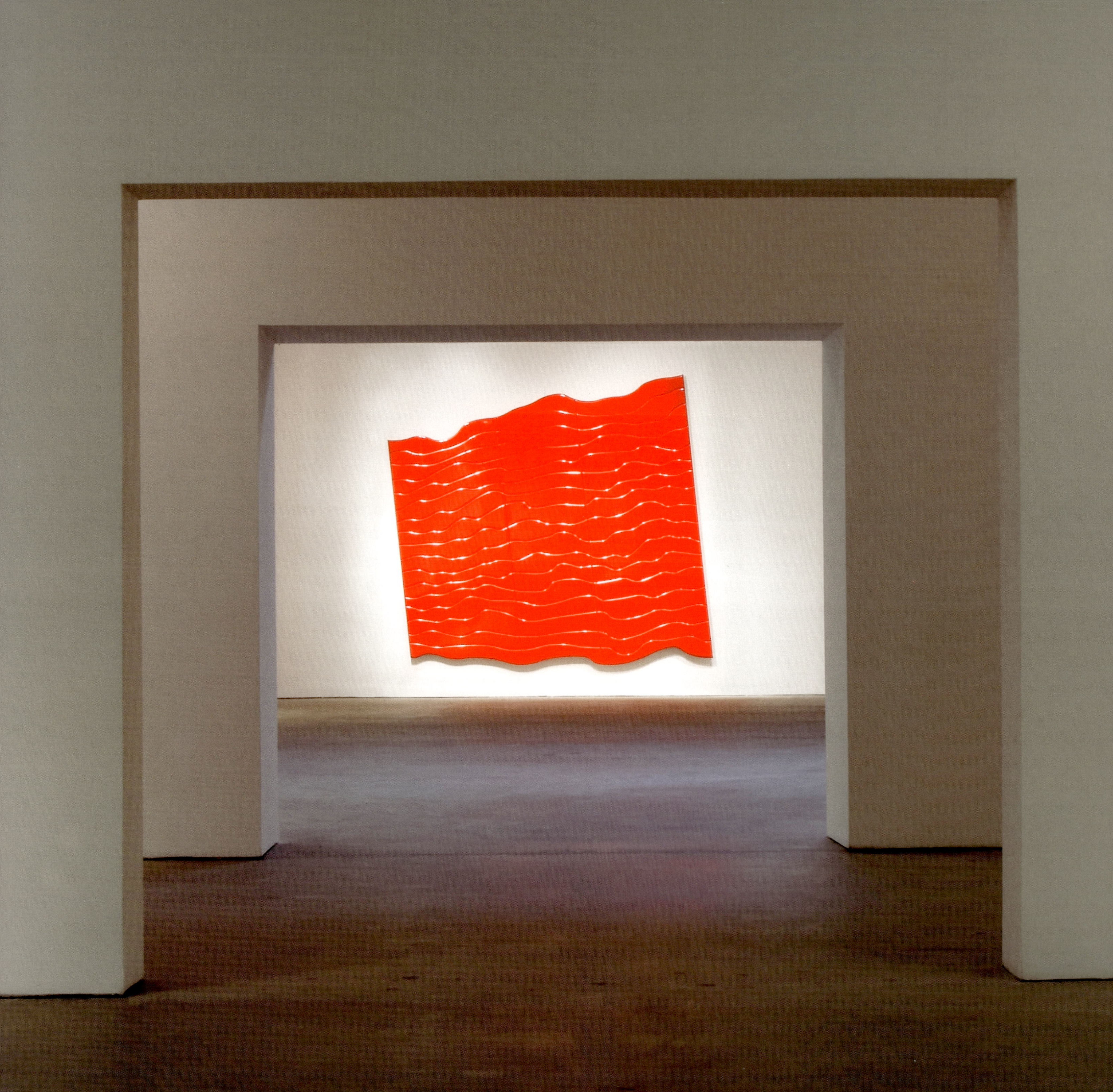

TERRA INCOGNITA

SCALE HAS ALWAYS BEEN A CONCERN FOR PAUL SARKISIAN, both visually and conceptually. Although it often appears overpowering, it is never arbitrary because for Sarkisian, scale is a primary catalyst by which we are made cognizant of our perceptual capabilities. The major scale of the artist's early representational façade series, including *Untitled (El Paso)* [plate 1] from the 1970s, for instance, corresponds to the composed realities of the buildings that each one depicts, as their size literally equates to their architectural dimensions. No longer demonstrating that our perception produces the finite scale of our physical world, his new body of nonobjective work inverts this logic so as to visualize the potential of the infinite, where scale is not restricted by linear dimensions. By questioning the a priori assumptions that constitute our paradigm of visual perception, Sarkisian reconfigures scale and reality so that they cease to be the mirrored elements of our ingrained axioms and in so doing discards the ruler as an adequate device for measurement.

Unbeknownst to Sarkisian, who rarely follows scientific developments, similar reconfigurations of our perceptual logic had been established as advanced theoretical principles in early-20th-century physics, when Isaac Newton's 1687 classical mechanics of objective reality were eroded by the velocity of Albert Einstein's theories of relativity, 1905-16. Newton's logic, which has been a part of our visual paradigm for centuries, incorporated Euclid's geometrical rigidity of dimension, as well as asserted that *time* was constant, *space* was flat, and that *time* and *space* had no effect on each other. Einstein turned this unbending construct into Jell-O by proposing that dimensional vectors undergo plastic transformations—*time* is relative, *space* distorts, and that *time* and *space* do have profound effects upon each other. This revolutionary shift, "visualized" as a series of mind-boggling equations, had no demonstrative effect on our preexisting perceptual notions because it was achievable only through the mathematical deductions of abstract thought. Ironically, as

opposite: *Untitled (red line51),* 2005, polyurethane on wood, 10' 11" x 12'

Sarkisian's methodology evolved from his earlier house and storefront canvases to this current body of work, he intuitively arrived at the finite/infinite conundrum that physics had "liberated" through the aforementioned series of arcane and so-called rational equations.

Sarkisian's approach was more humanistic in that he relied on our discerning constructs as the basis to achieve visual, rather than theoretical, propositions. As his starting point, Sarkisian used our perceptive consensus—staunchly proscribed in his earlier compositions—that equates visual reality to the reality of scale. Then, he inverted this logic by decoding its construction: its parts (*things*), its structure (*the vantage point*), and the result (*a snapshot*). In so doing, he realized that the conceptual-to-visual process by which we rationalize our finite reality is but half of this axiom. By inverting the presupposed order of its components, our visual maxim subsequently morphs into a primary *field* determined by its effect on the actions of things, rather than by the things themselves. This shift from snapshot to field is Sarkisian's lexicon, which enables us to conceive infinite spatial concepts while it gives physicists pictorial similes for their intangible hypothesis.

Though physics has in its way emancipated the visualization of the infinite, our visual reality remains grounded in the perception of physical things experienced from one vantage point. The result is a still-life snapshot that represents a static moment in space and time. As more things accumulate, the larger the snapshot becomes, and, with each infinitesimal shift of our eyes, another is created. The relationship between things within the snapshot—i.e. the layered distance of perspective defined by the composite of height, width, and length—describes the three-dimensionality of our reality. The accumulation of these snapshots sequentially forms the linear panorama of our measurable reality and defines who, what, and where we are. While these cinematic frames substantiate the day-to-day resolution of our finite world, they have also blindsided us into visual complacency.

By conceptually pushing the brittle infrastructure of this logic through a sieve, Sarkisian arrived at its malleable other half. Through this filtering process, he challenges our reliance on the rigidity of spatial vectors (top, bottom, left, right); the locational fix of perspective (near, far); and the linear sequencing of the static snapshot. The hierarchy of interest—things placed within the visual priorities of layering—is of equal importance when this short-sighted dimensionality is transposed and the static moment of time inverts to the fluid *space/time continuum*, also referred to as the fourth dimension. The result is a nonrestrictive field that correlates to, but does not mirror, the inverted half's snapshot. No longer confined to a static three-dimensional format, the field, in continuous flux and expansion, serves as the matrix for the ceaseless interfacing of energy and tension that determines the behavior of the things which occupy it. This continuously mutating interaction between energy and materiality is Sarkisian's visual mapping of the infinite, and though it may appear as the terra incognita of an unfocused cartographer, it is the conceptual extrapolation of our measurable reality into an evolving continuum of the immeasurable.

The artist's *Untitled (El Paso)*, 1971–72, appears to verify our measurable reality, yet it subversively alters our three-dimensional visual templates, while the work from four decades later (1992–2005), comprising the fields of Sarkisian's ideological inversion, fully transitions this development and triggers contemplation of what is beyond, behind, and within. The scale of these works is usurped by their conceptual infinities. This exhibition presents the aesthetic impetus for Sarkisian's questioning while charting the evolution of his visual forecasting.

The all-in-focus picture planes of the pivotal façade series give them a hyper-clarity that is foreign to our perceptive reality. Even though this manipulation was primarily used to heighten the visual experience of these canvases, Sarkisian unconsciously alluded to Einstein's proposition relating to the spatial compression of objects as a corollary to increased momentum, thereby warping our visual reality into the fluidity of the continuum. Within the rigorous visual logic of these earlier works, their mimetic realities clearly indicate that Sarkisian was, at the outset, already questioning the assumptions of our finite visual truths.

Following the stasis of *Untitled (El Paso)*'s snapshot, the first works pushed through Sarkisian's conceptual sieve—beginning with *Untitled (copper dot3)*, 1992 [plate 23], and concluding with *Untitled (blue8, shape2)*, 1999 [plate 11]—invert that inertia. While the perspective in *Untitled (El Paso)* is subtly compressed, it is squeezed out completely in these later works. Since time is no longer static, the upheaval occurring in these fields is filled with chaotic energy, as the objects in *Untitled (El Paso)* are reconfigured into the nonreferential flecks of contrasting color that flow across their surfaces. The jagged, translucent shapes that puncture the field of *Untitled (white mark/black/vertical3)*, 1994 [plate 22], articulate the "stressed and strained" distortions of change as they are forcibly transformed and absorbed into its tension. As the field harnesses the unruly marks that occupy it, the resulting energy manifests a dynamic harmony, as in *Untitled (blue8, shape2)* where increasingly uniform shapes are thereby held in an orderly, pulsating network across the surface.

Sarkisian's fields are constantly re-assimilating the things that fill them, reducing their composition into finer and more highly charged specks of matter. In works such as *Untitled (orange32),* 2000 [plate 10], and *Untitled (silver27)*, 2004 [plate 12], the flecks are now compressed into dense layers of iridescent dust which intermittently appear and disappear into the field's flux of intense color. Their highly polished surfaces emphasize the liquidity of their multidirectional flow. Works such as *Untitled (magenta16)*, 2003 [plate 20], and *Untitled (multicolor32)*, 2004 [plate 25], accentuate the field's transformative effect as disparate colors temporarily coexist before being synchronized in hue and intensity.

Until 2005, the size and shape of the panels within the artist's grids have been uniform, either squares or rectangles, which give semblance to the fluctuating activity occurring within the work. These familiar formats, however, extend the experiential process to the conception of infinite expansion; while their structures simulate our planar reality, their massive scale extends beyond our peripheral vision. Consequently, edges no longer exist as the encroaching tensions of their fluid fields spill infinitely in all directions.

While aspects of Sarkisian's conceptual inversion remain present, the works created in 2005 make some dramatic twists. Although their flux of pure color remains consistent with his methodology, their shape and scale do not. By reducing their scale, as well as shifting from more traditional formats to shaped configurations (both external and internal), these works deconstruct the earlier field inversions by graphically visualizing the distortions of energy transference between the field and things that occupy it. As a result, they are the purest manifestations of Sarkisian's ideology. In these works, the artist has literally joined both ends of his conceptual sieve by juxtaposing finite reality and infinite fields. These juxtapositions highlight the erosion of our visual insistence on things. The curved eddies that circumscribe *Untitled (left leaning yellow51)*, 2005 [page 12], for example, are both positively defined by the field and negatively outlined by the finite reality of its placement. Within this context, the work's surging motion eclipses the static moment; its swirling field inverts the motionless perspective of an object against a wall into elliptical forces of expanding unrest.

The unexpected wavelike configurations of *Untitled (concave15)*, 2005 [plate 9]—the artist's most recent work—may appear as a "blip" in Sarkisian's ideological evolution, but they fit comfortably within his conceptual inversion. This work also provides a visual analogy to physics's ongoing revisions relating to field formation. As his uncanny intuition continues to visually connote science's abstracted theories, the structure of *Untitled (concave15)* coincides with quantum theory's 1928 hypothesis of wave motions in space, which was implied, but not clarified, in Einstein's general theory of relativity. This hypothesis proposes that fields are the result of the interactions that occur between their ebb and flow. The concave fields in Sarkisian's piece—the first of his to have multiple fields—are the result of this "push and pull" exchange as they ripple into infinity.

Sarkisian's work has always questioned our perceptions of reality. By brilliantly exploiting our a priori visual paradigm, he provides compelling strategies that allow us to understand its restrictive assumptions, as well as the conceptual tools to visualize those realities that are beyond our static moment. Without a doubt, Sarkisian's *fields* map terra incognita's far-distant shores—but they are more the focused mapping of perceived infinity.

—CHRISTOPHER CORDES
New York, 2005

Christopher Cordes is a writer and artist currently living in New York City.
He is a Tamarind Master Printer, Tamarind Institute, College of Fine Arts, University of New Mexico. He also compiled the catalogue raisonné Bruce Nauman Prints 1970–1989 *(copublished by the Leo Castelli, Lawrence/Monk, and Donald Young galleries; 1989).*

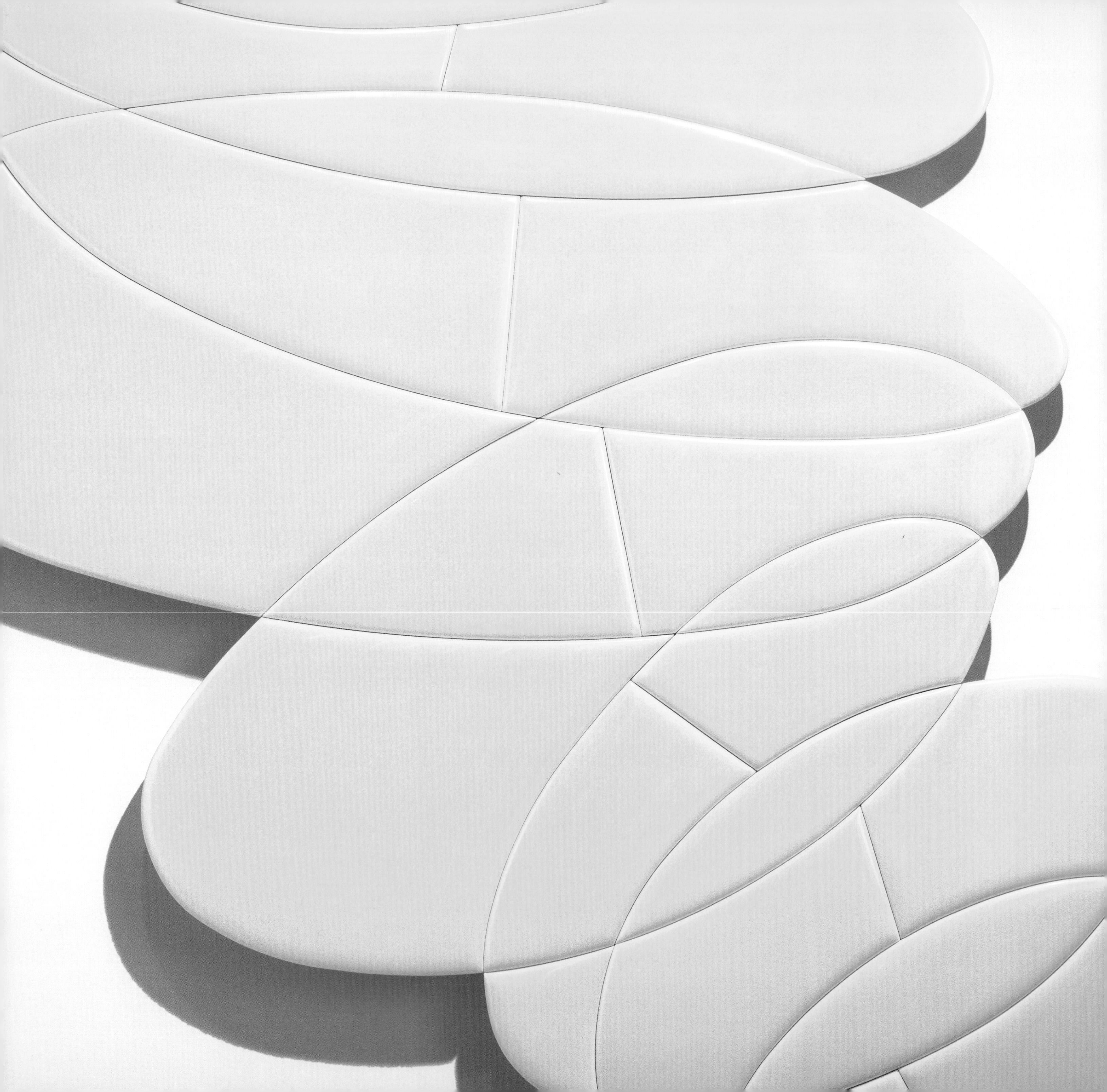

PLATES

1 *Untitled (El Paso)*, 1971–72, acrylic on canvas, 14' × 21'

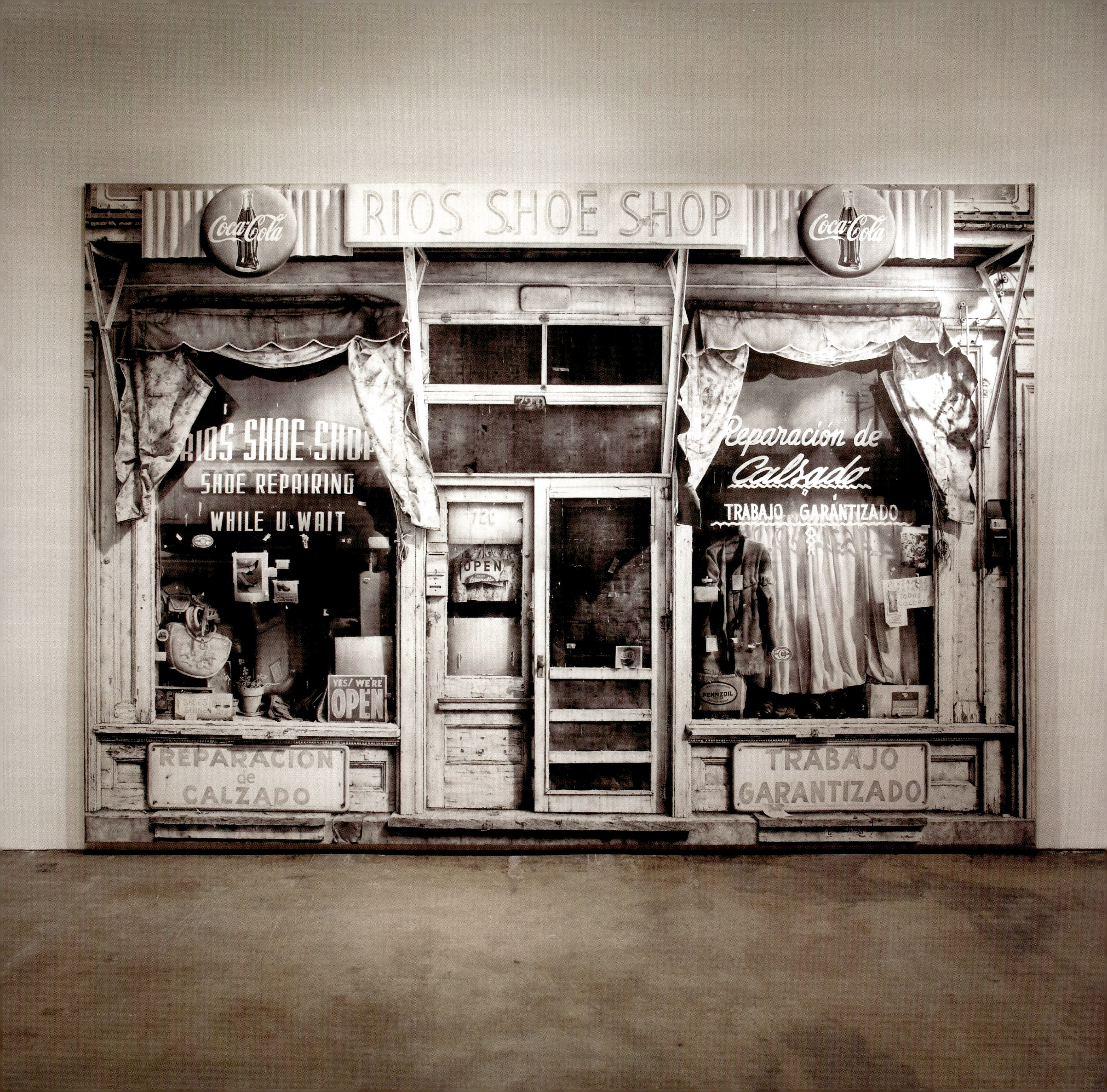

RIOS SHOE SHOP
Coca-Cola
Coca-Cola
RIOS SHOE SHOP
SHOE REPAIRING
WHILE U WAIT
Reparación de
Calzado
TRABAJO GARANTIZADO
OPEN
YES! WE'RE
OPEN
PENNZOIL
REPARACION
de
CALZADO
TRABAJO
GARANTIZADO

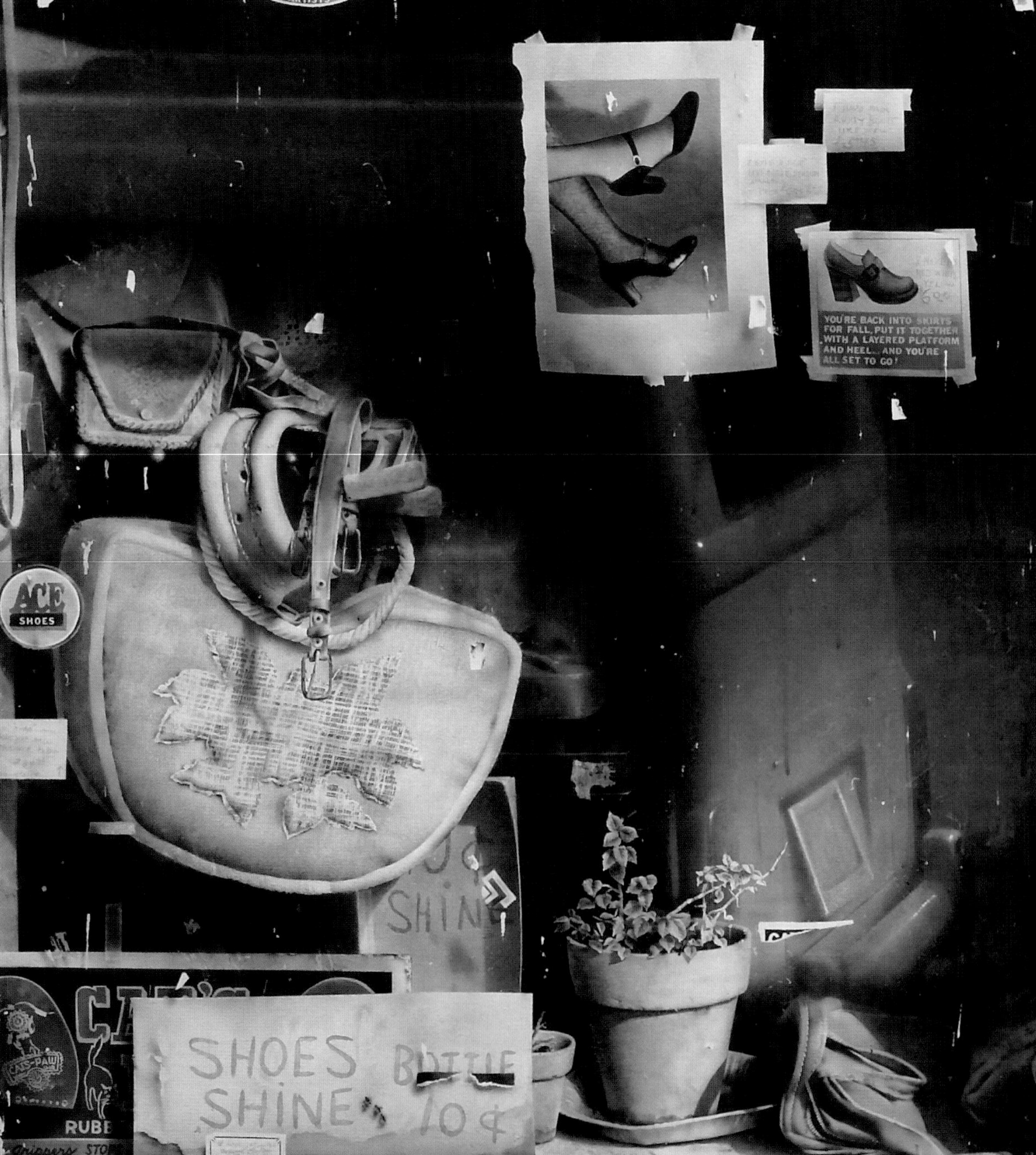
SHOE REPAIRING
WHILE U WAIT
NAT. FED. OF INDEPENDENT
VOTING MEMBER
ARTISTS
YOU'RE BACK INTO SKIRTS FOR FALL, PUT IT TOGETHER WITH A LAYERED PLATFORM AND HEEL... AND YOU'RE ALL SET TO GO!
ACE
SHOES
SHOES SHINE
YES! WE'RE
OPEN

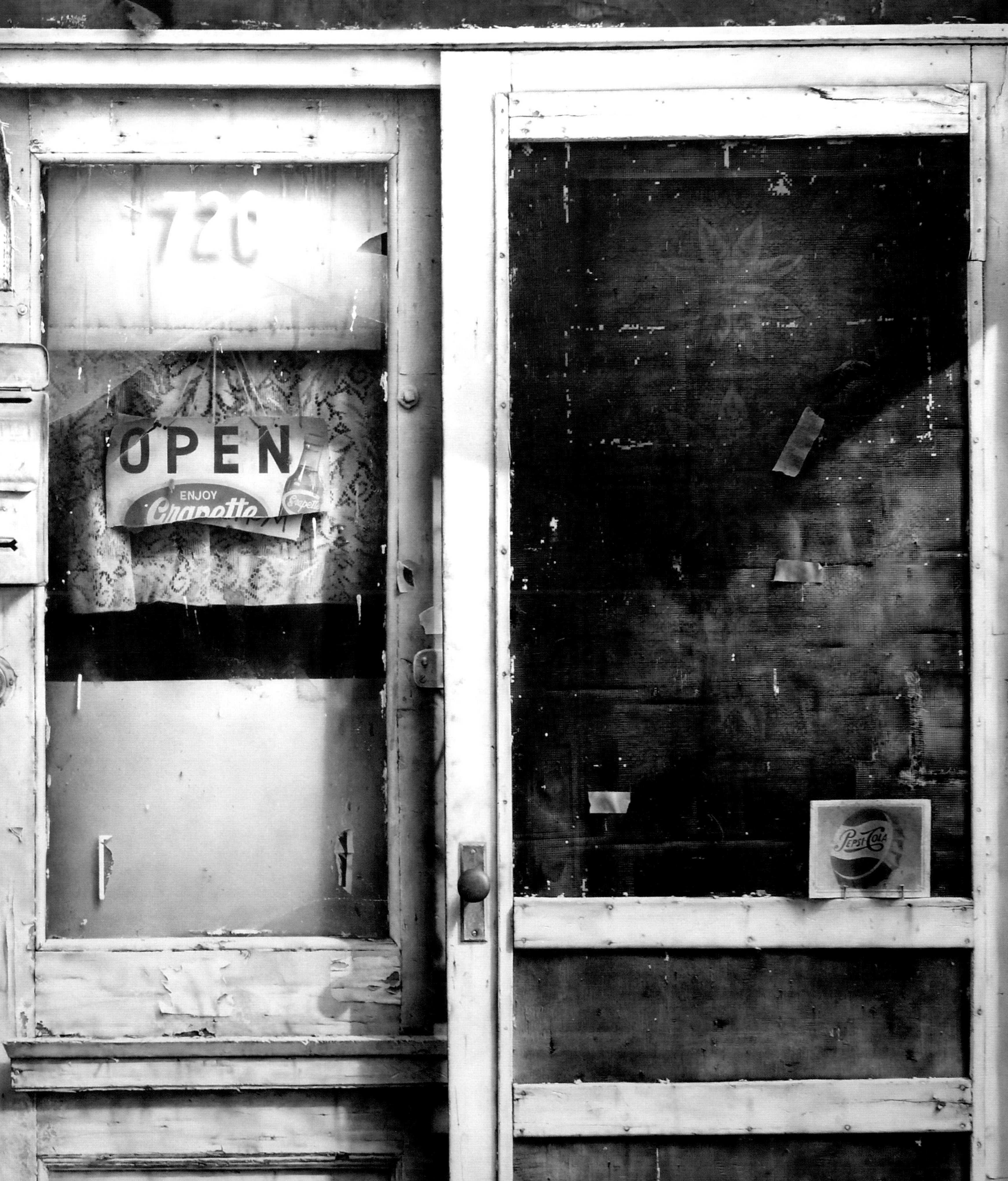
720
OPEN
ENJOY
Grapette
Pepsi-Cola

2 *Untitled (white line51)*, 2005, polyurethane on wood, 10' 11" × 12'

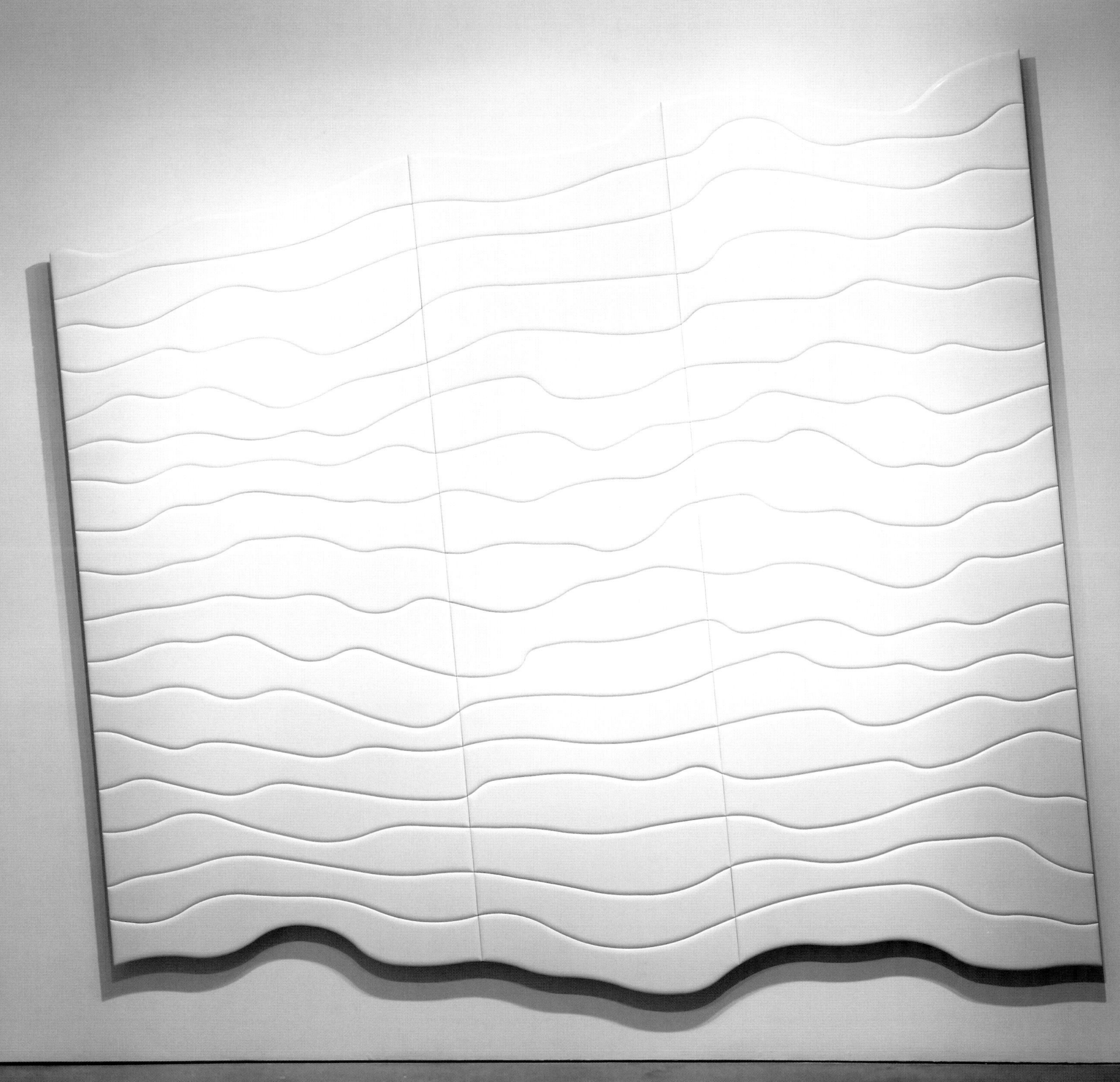

3 *Untitled (bronze/green42)*, 2005, polyurethane on wood, 6' 5" × 11' 8"

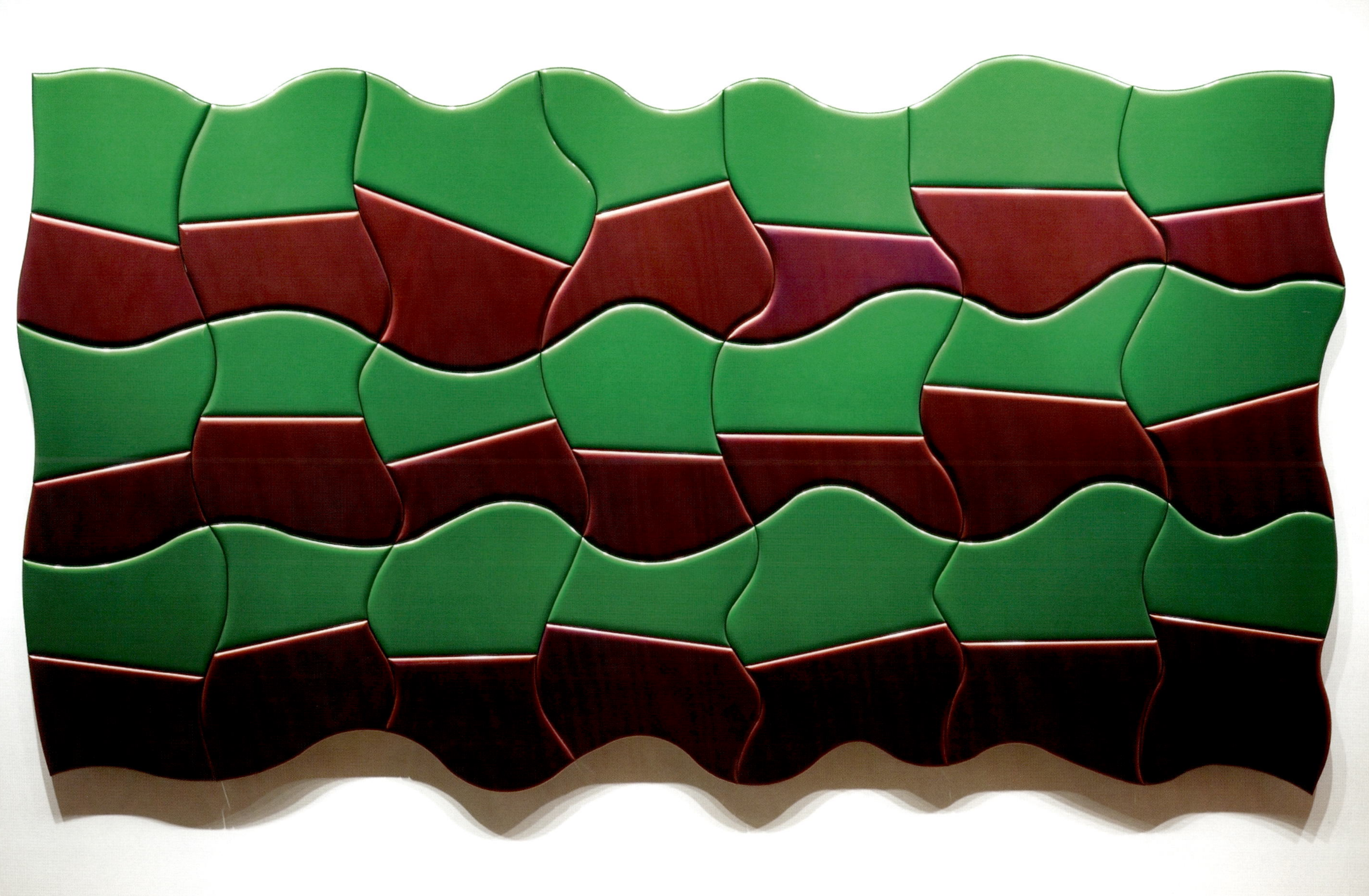

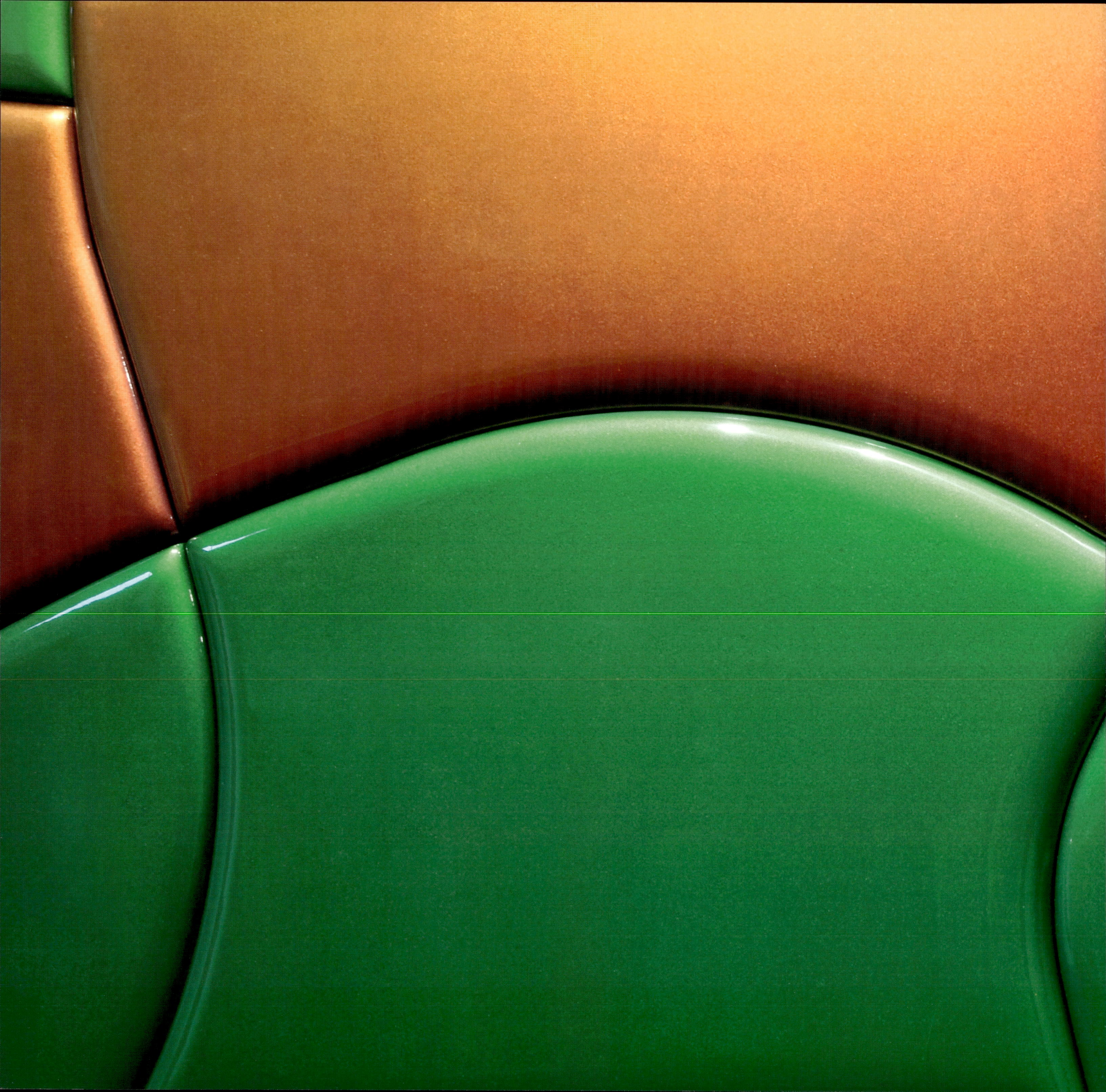

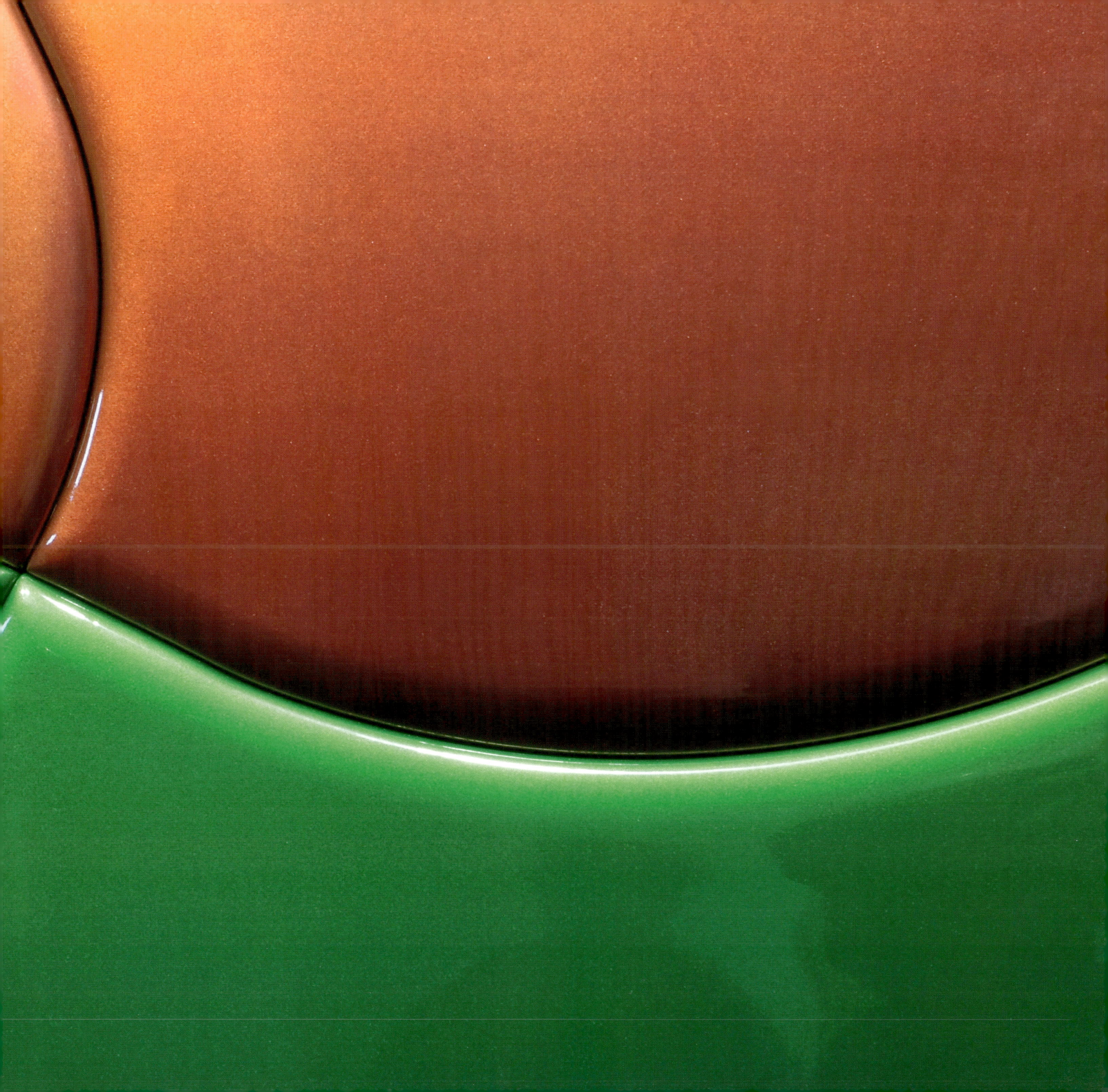

4 *Untitled (multicolor line51)*, 2005, polyurethane on wood, 12' × 10' 11"

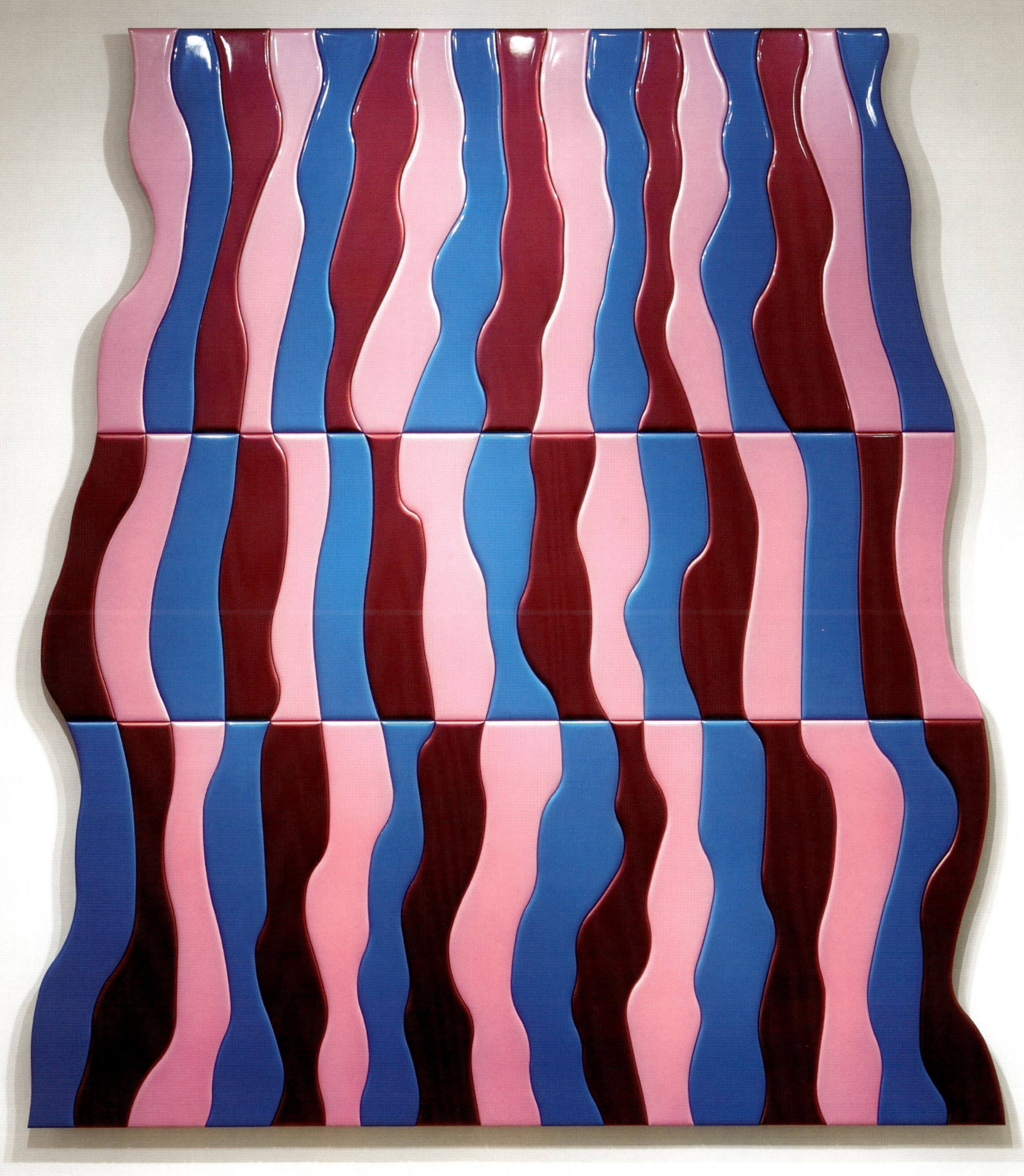

5 *Untitled (red line51)*, 2005, polyurethane on wood, 10' 11" × 12'

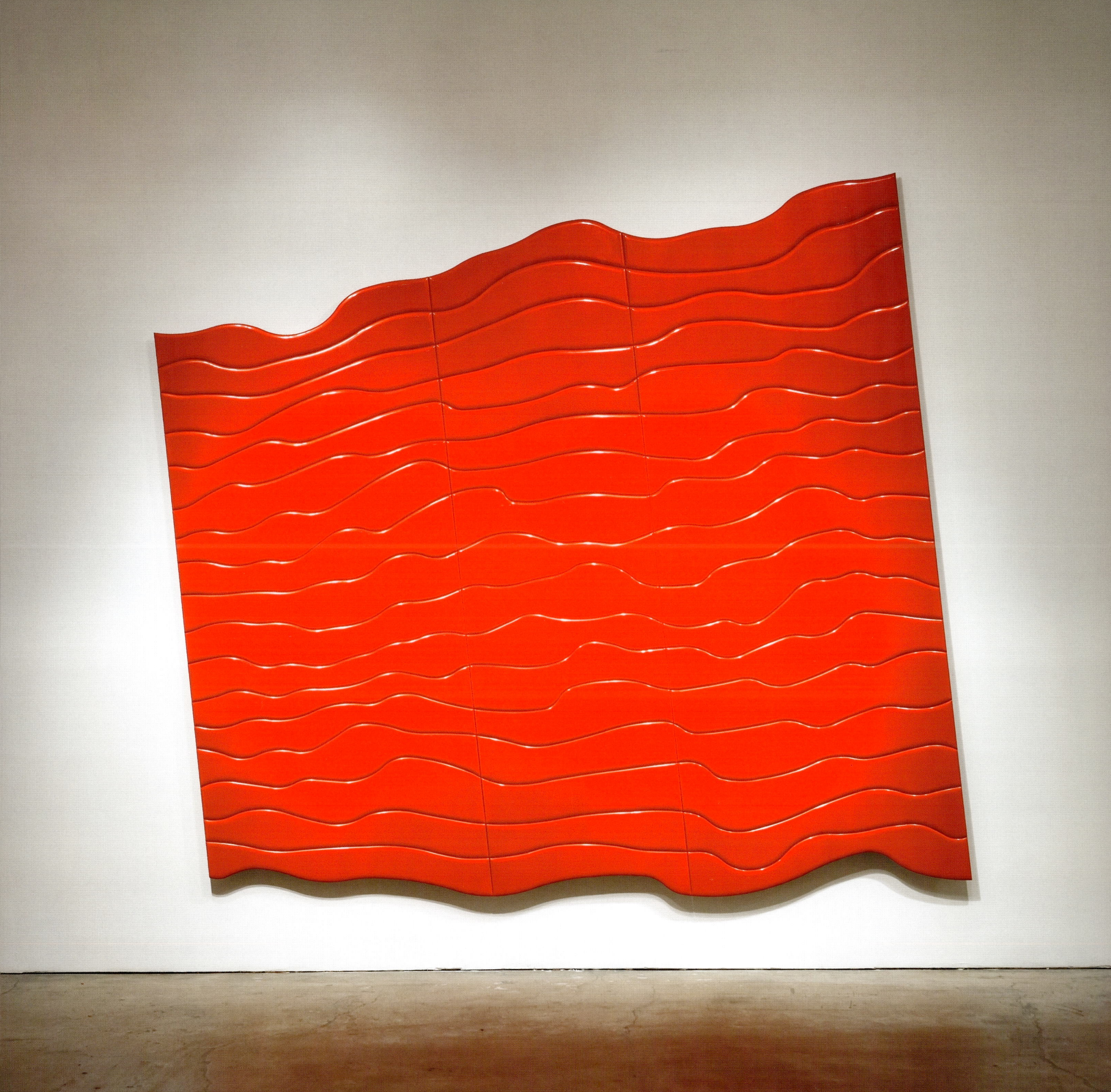

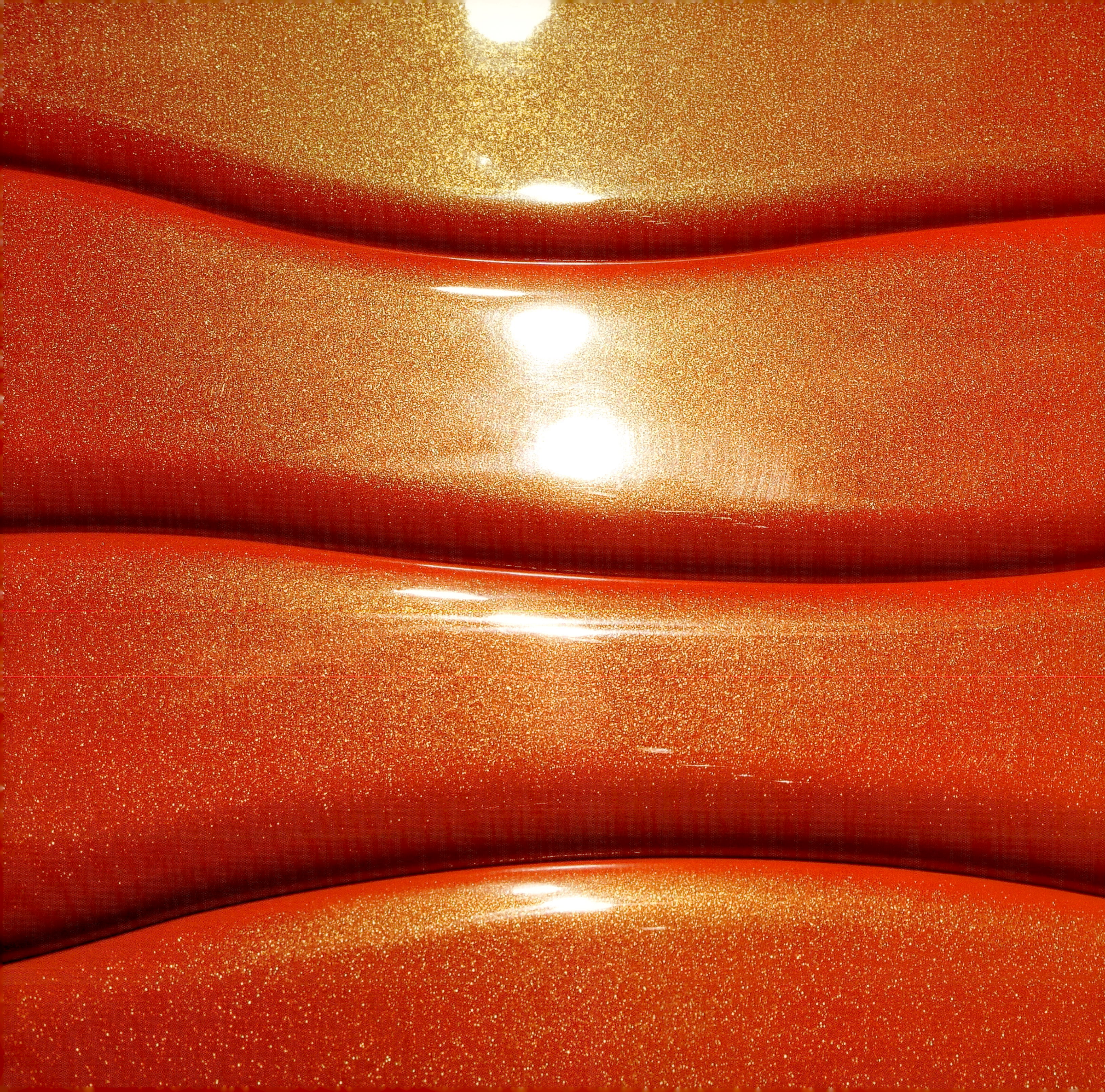

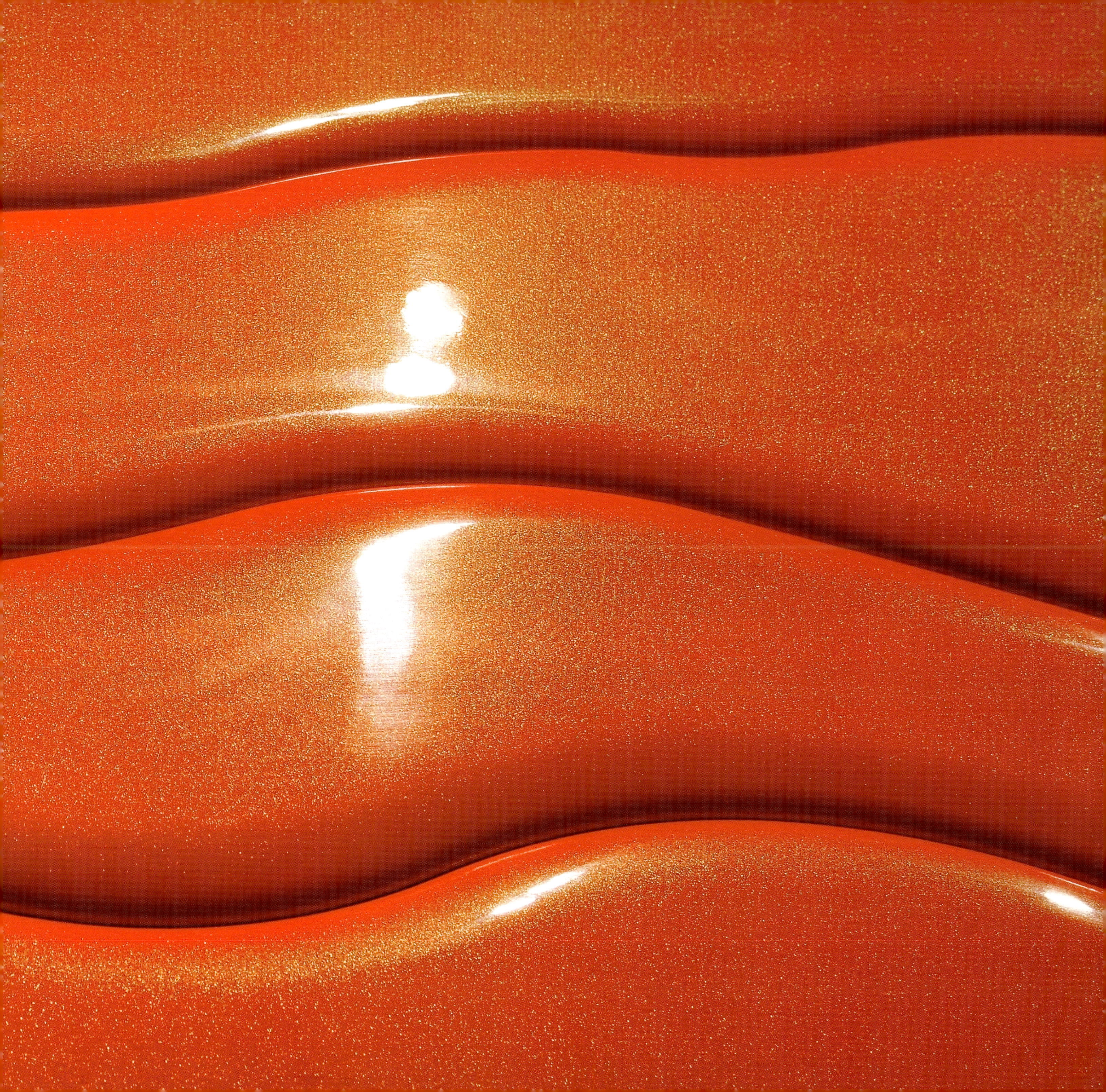

6 *Untitled (blue/yellow42)*, 2005, polyurethane on wood, 11' 8" × 6' 5"

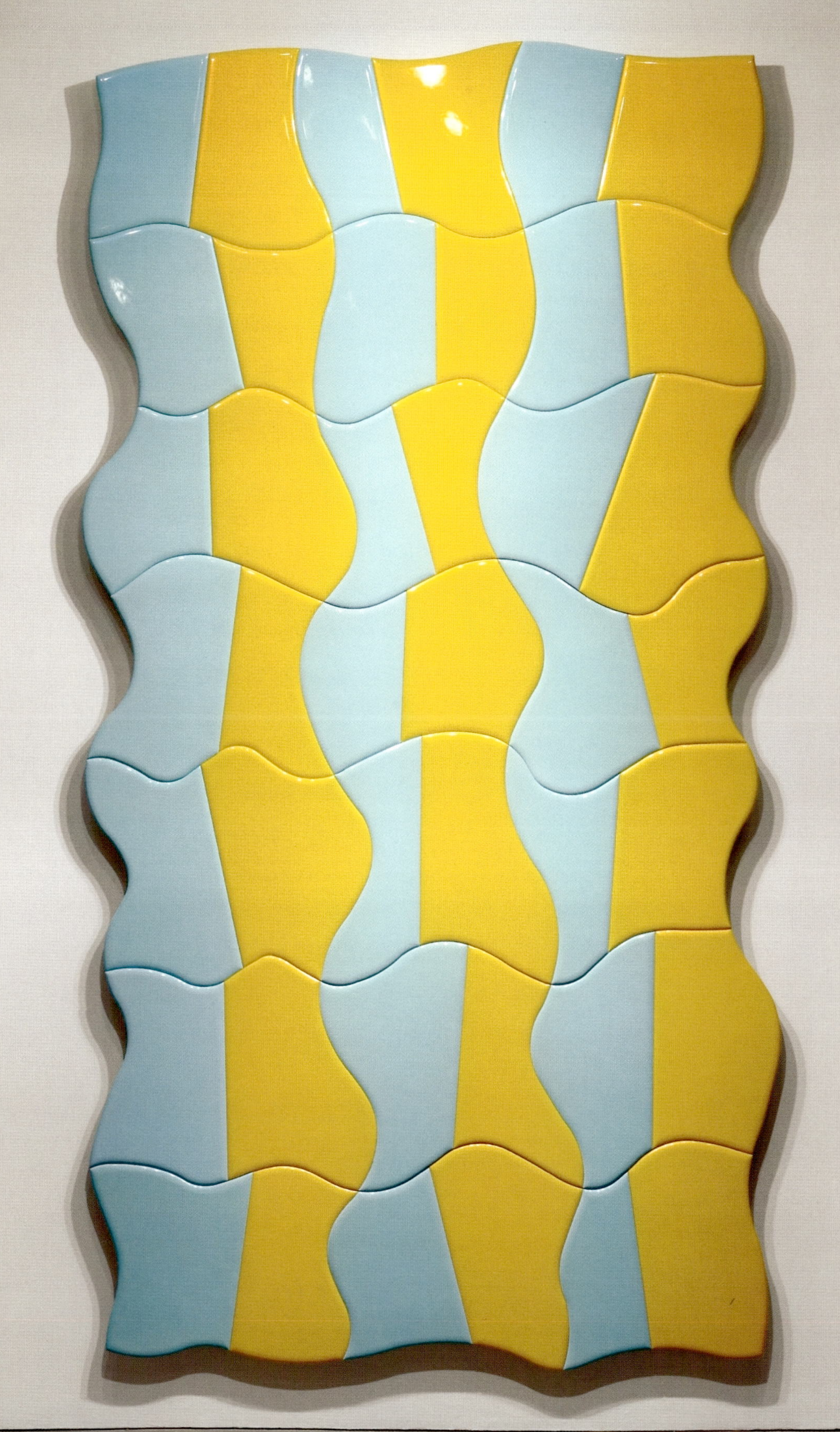

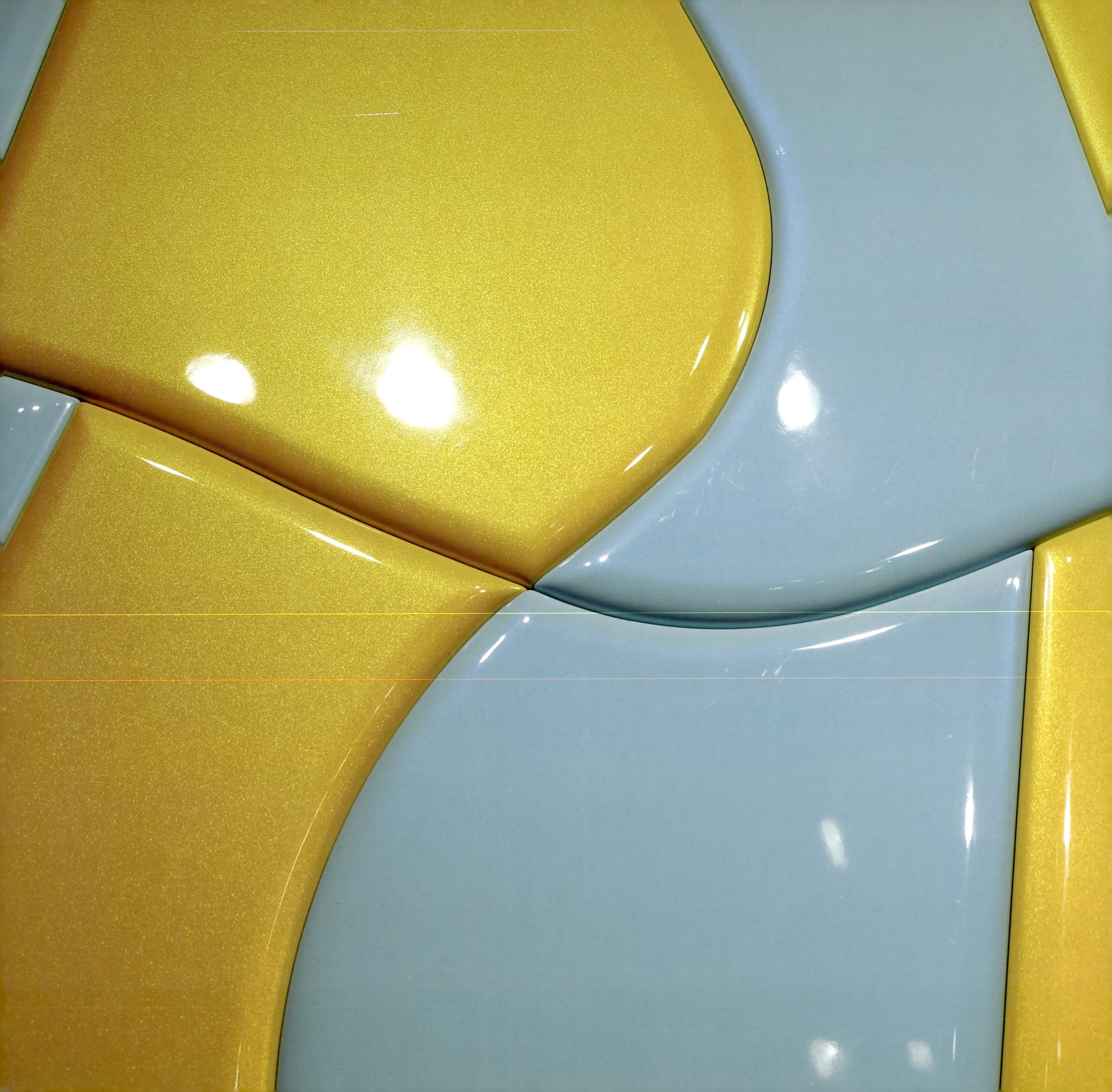

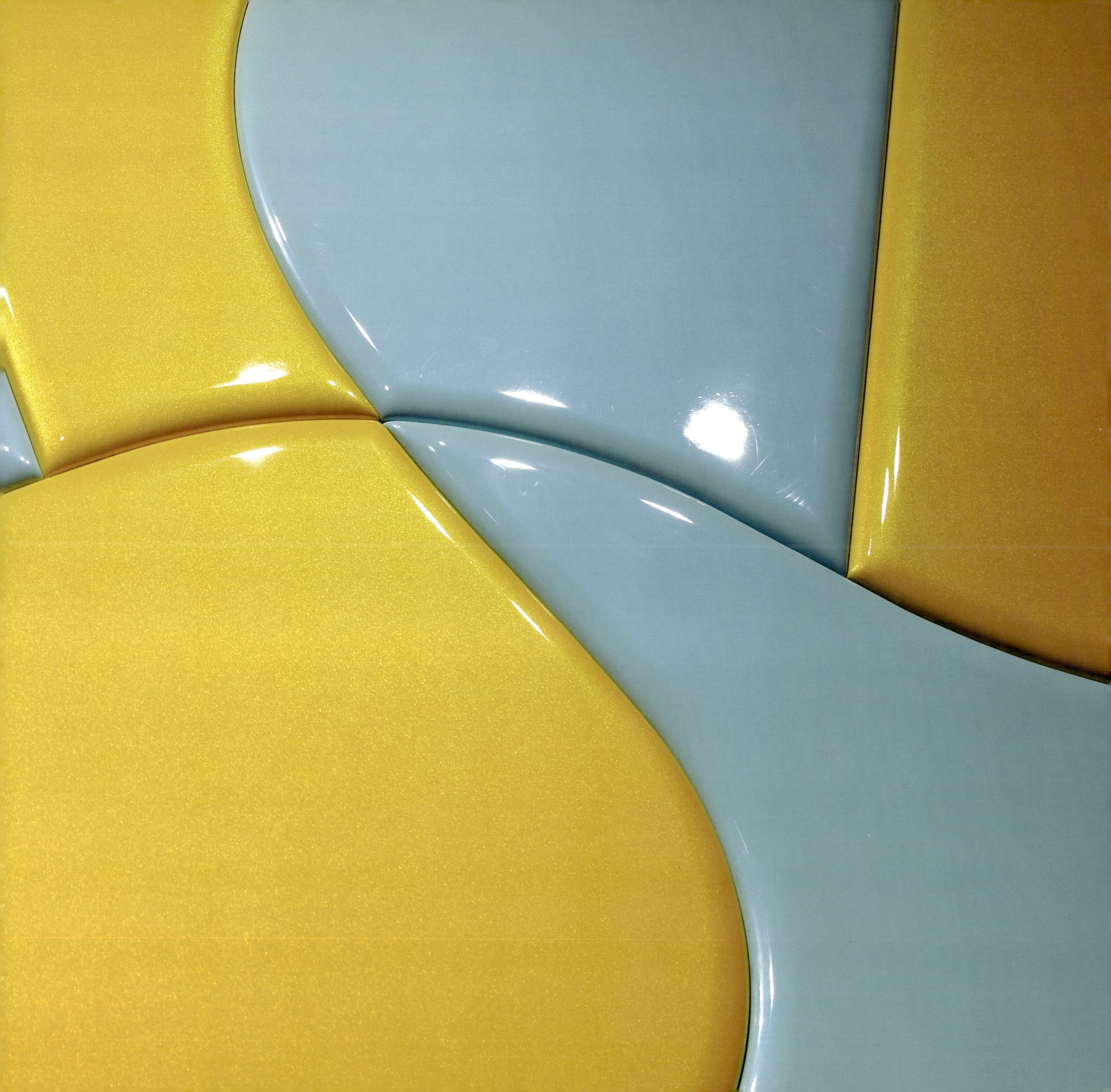

7 *Untitled (right leaning red51)*, 2005, polyurethane on wood, 14' × 7' 5"

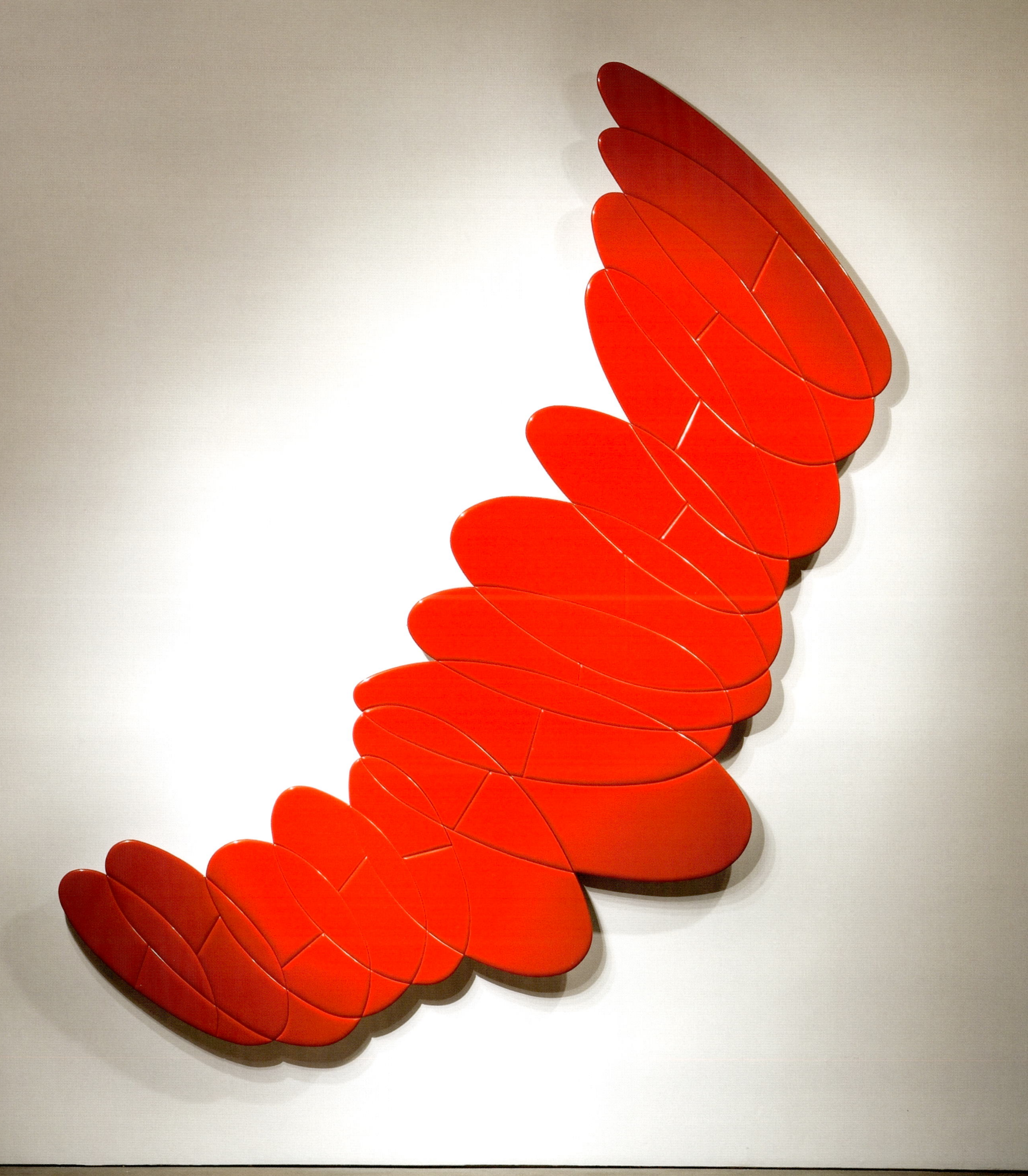

8 | *Untitled (silver16)*, 2004, polyurethane on wood, 12' × 12'

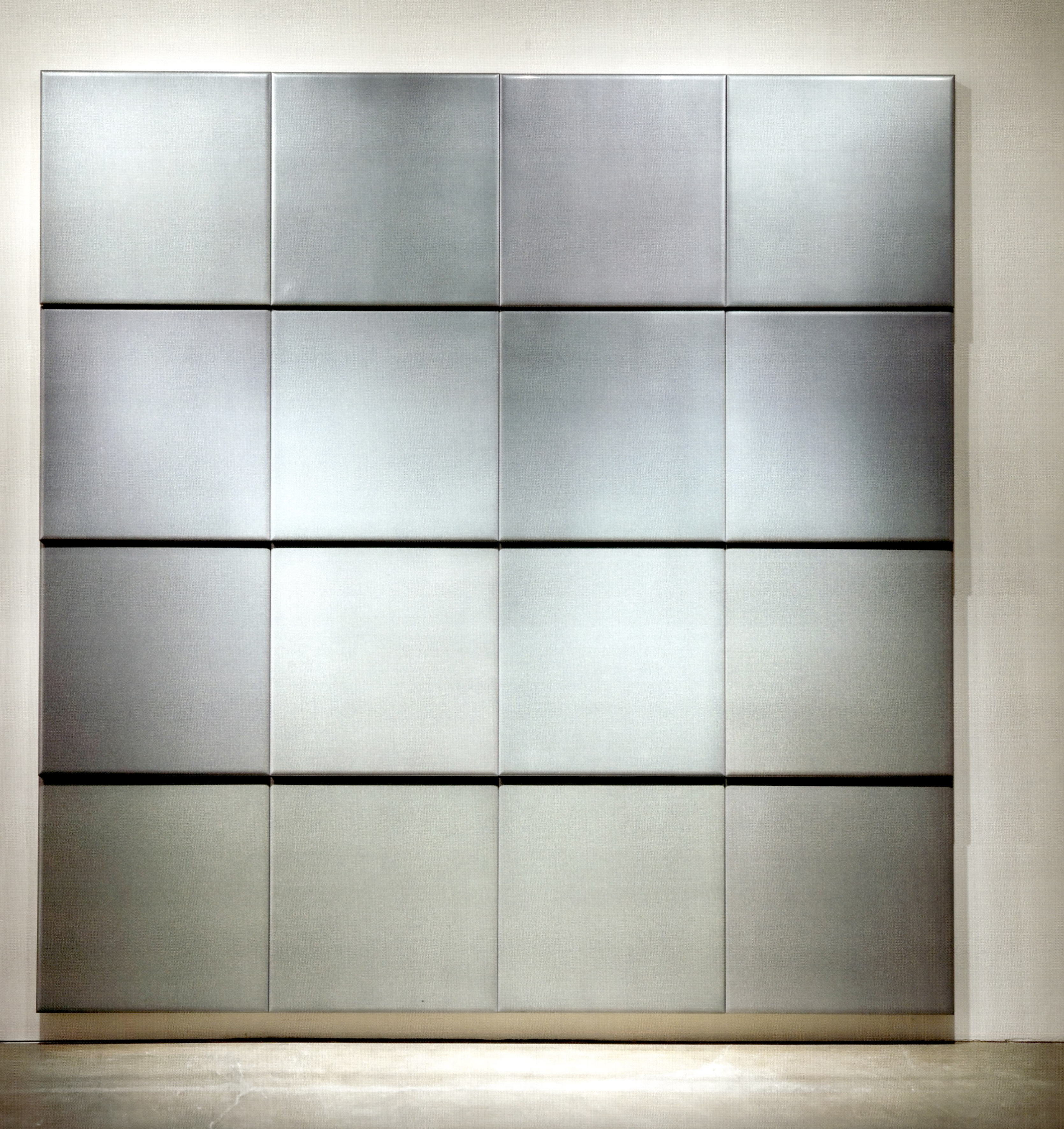

9 *Untitled (concave15)*, 2005, polyurethane on wood, 8' × 12' 6"

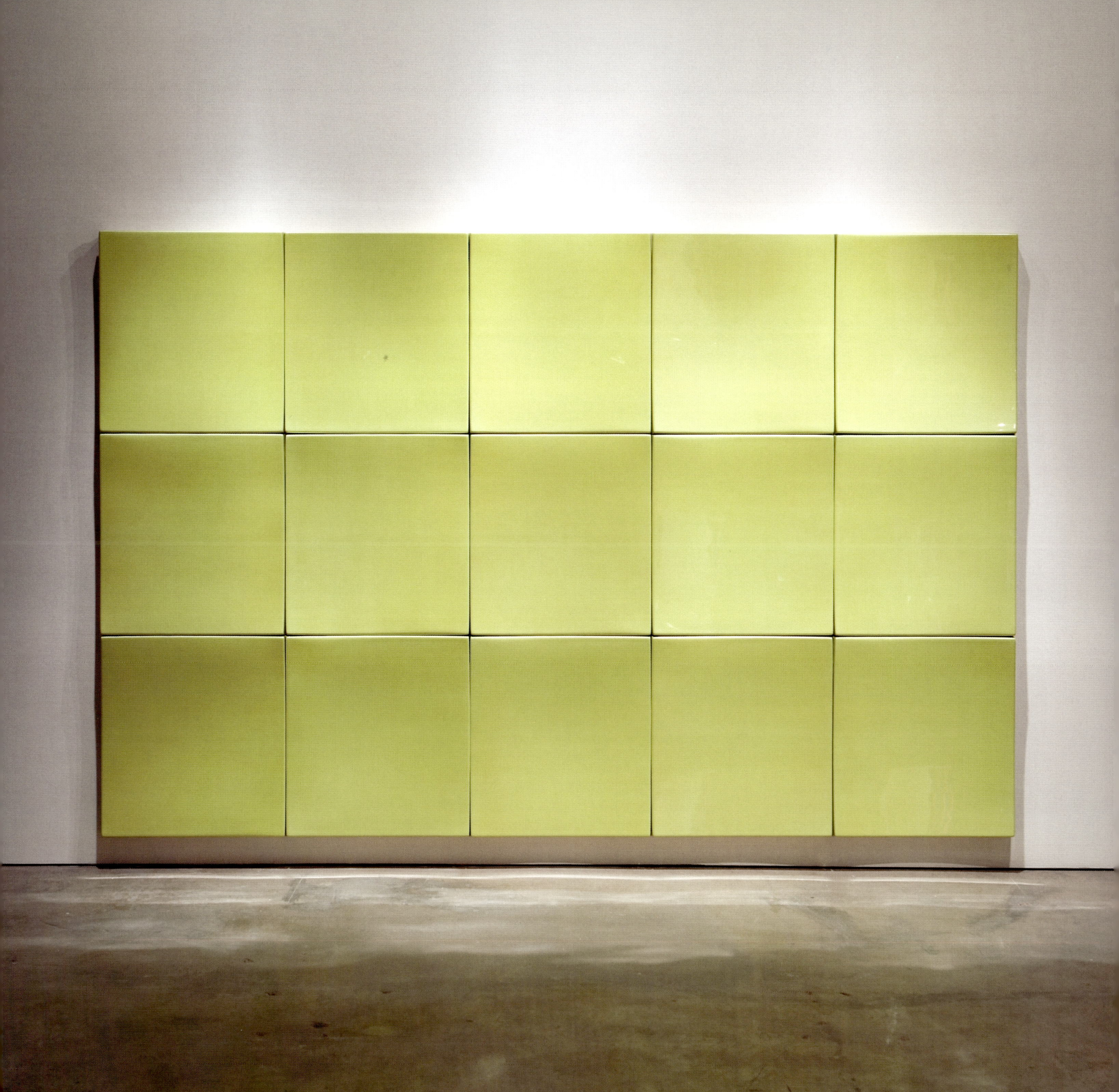

10 | *Untitled (orange32)*, 2000, polyurethane on wood, 12' x 24'

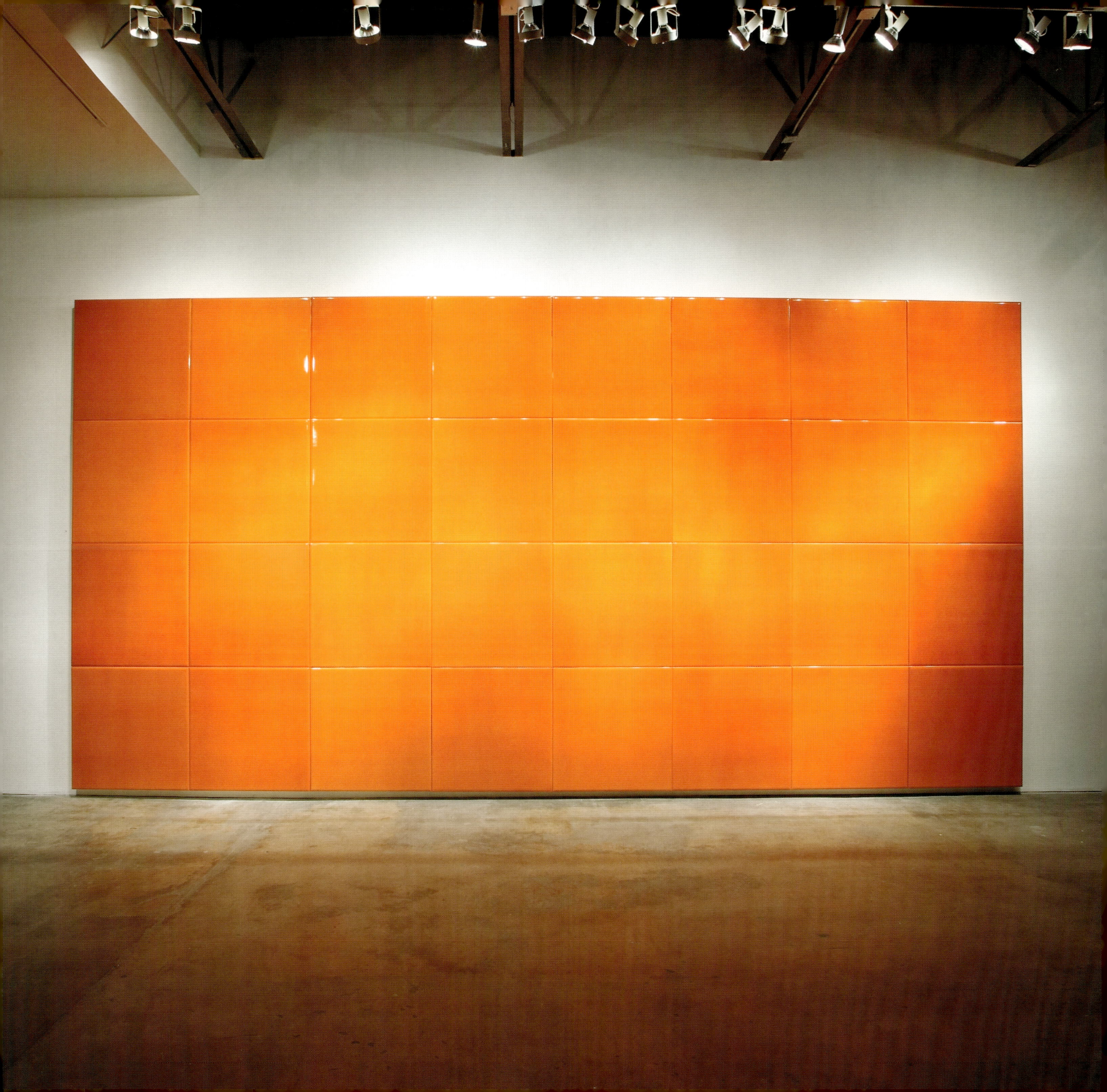

11 | *Untitled (blue8, shape2)*, 1999, resin epoxy on wood, 10' × 25'

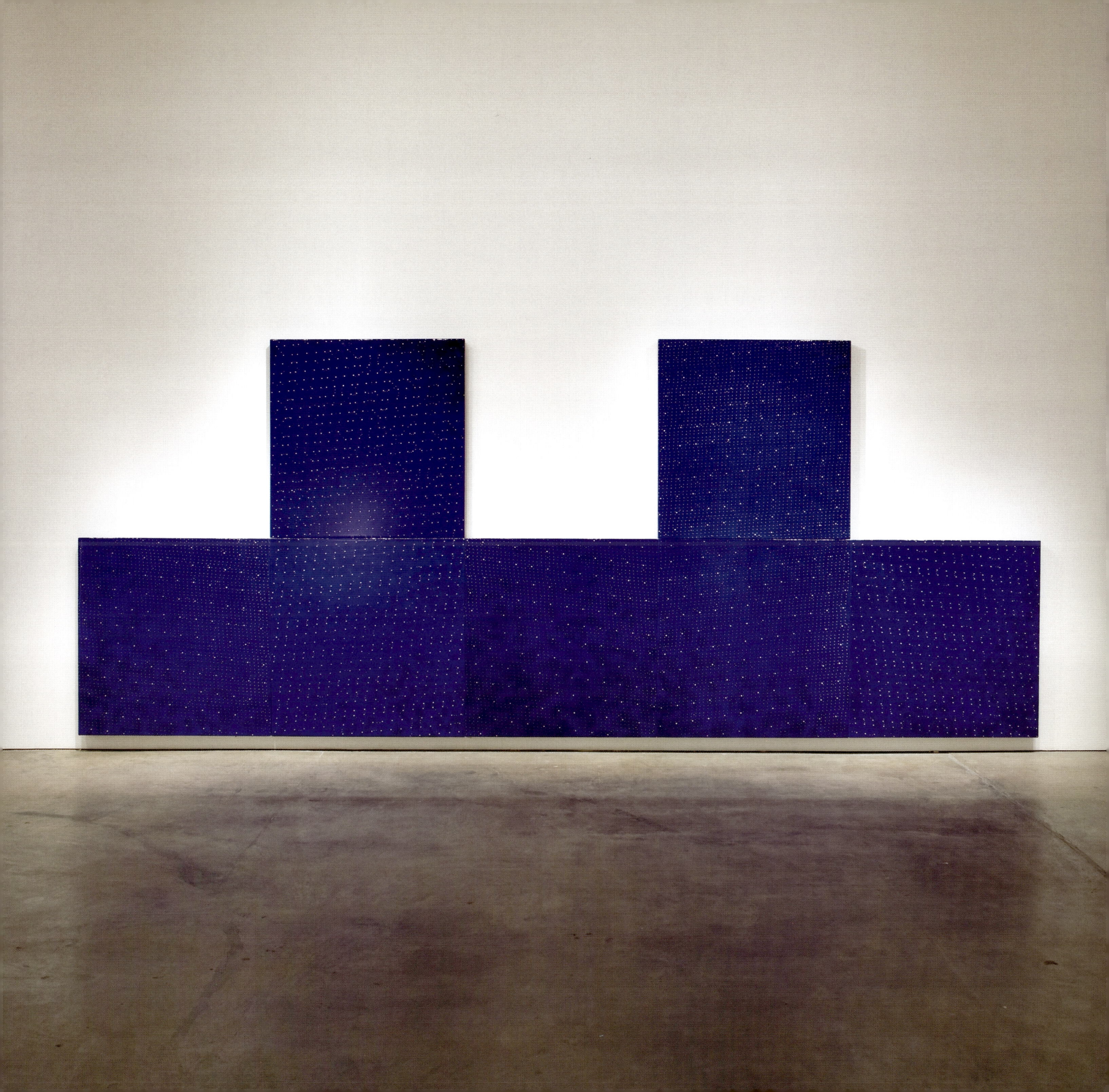

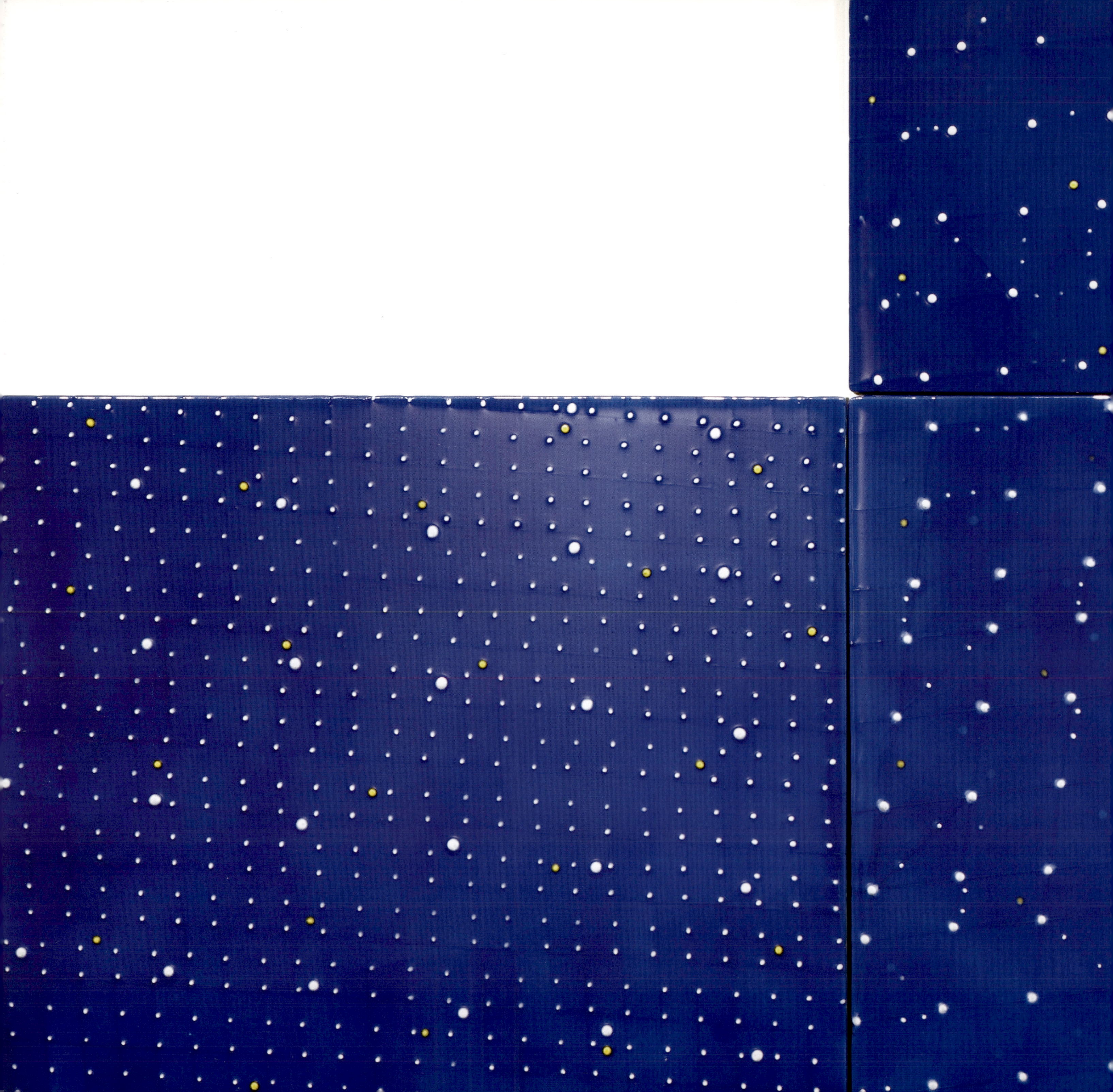

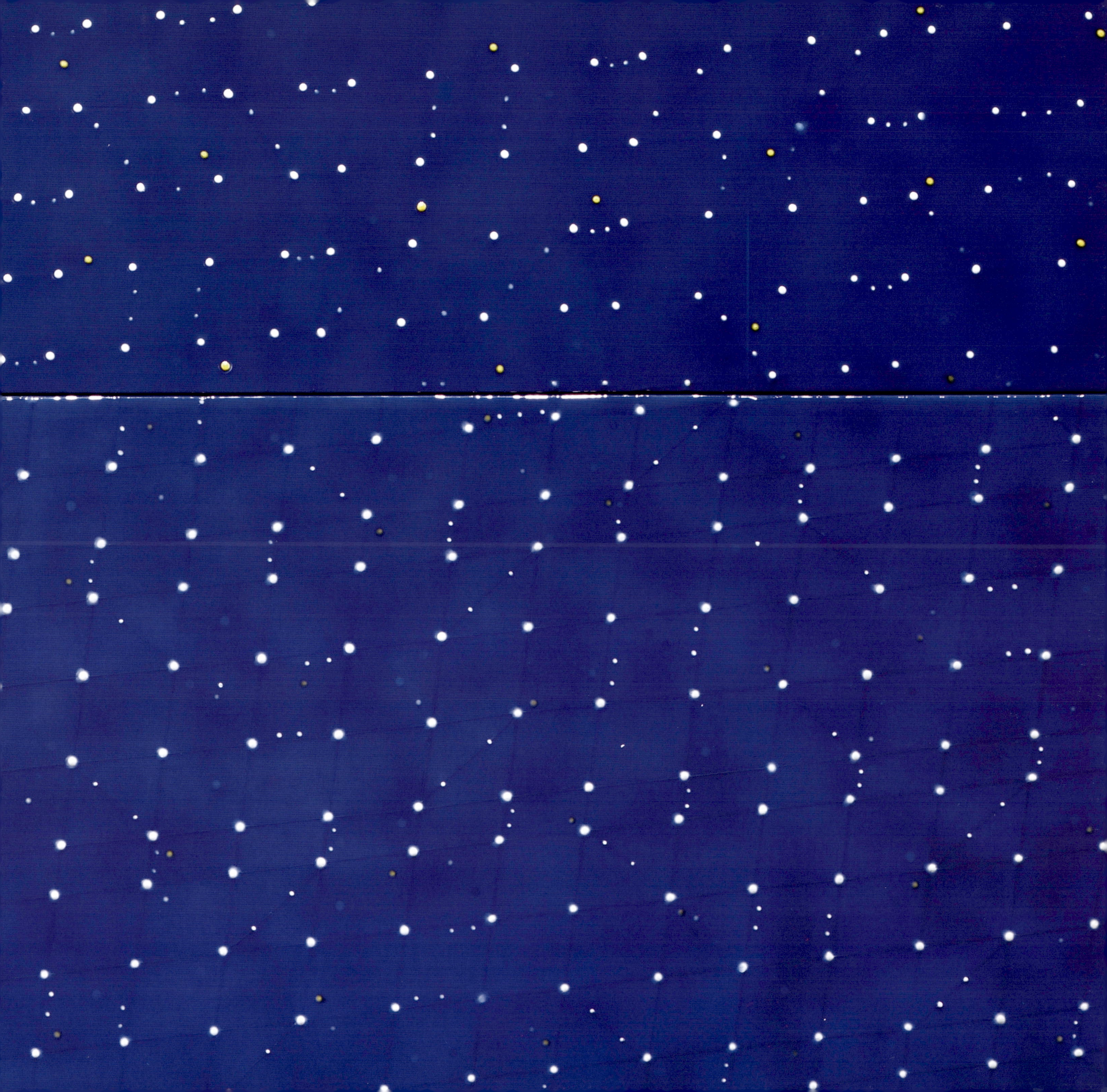

12 *Untitled (silver27)*, 2004, polyurethane on wood, 8' 7" × 12'

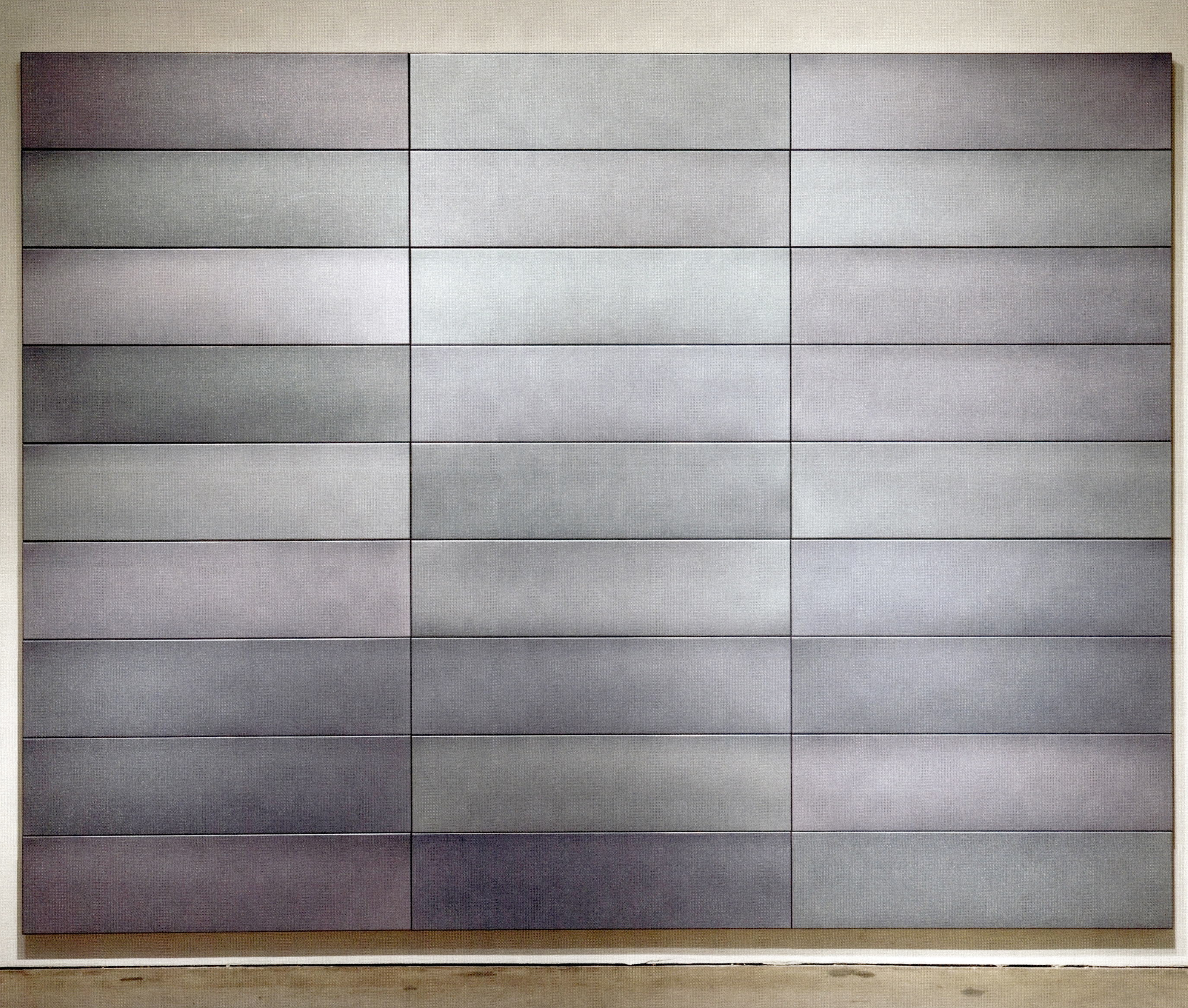

13 *Untitled (light blue8)*, 2001, polyurethane on wood, 12' × 6'

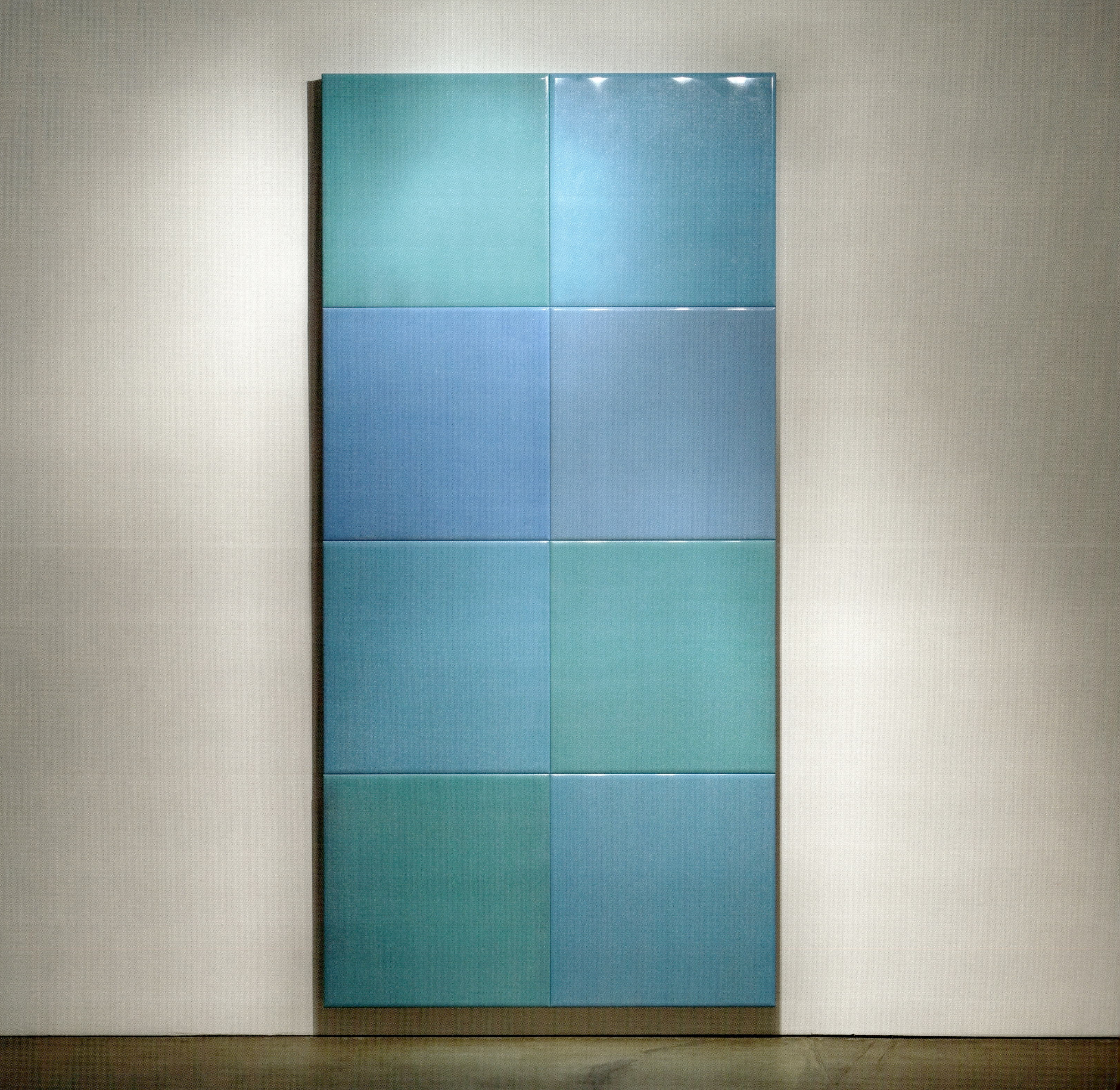

14 *Untitled (light yellow panel)*, 2005, polyurethane on fiberglass, 6' 9" × 4' 11"

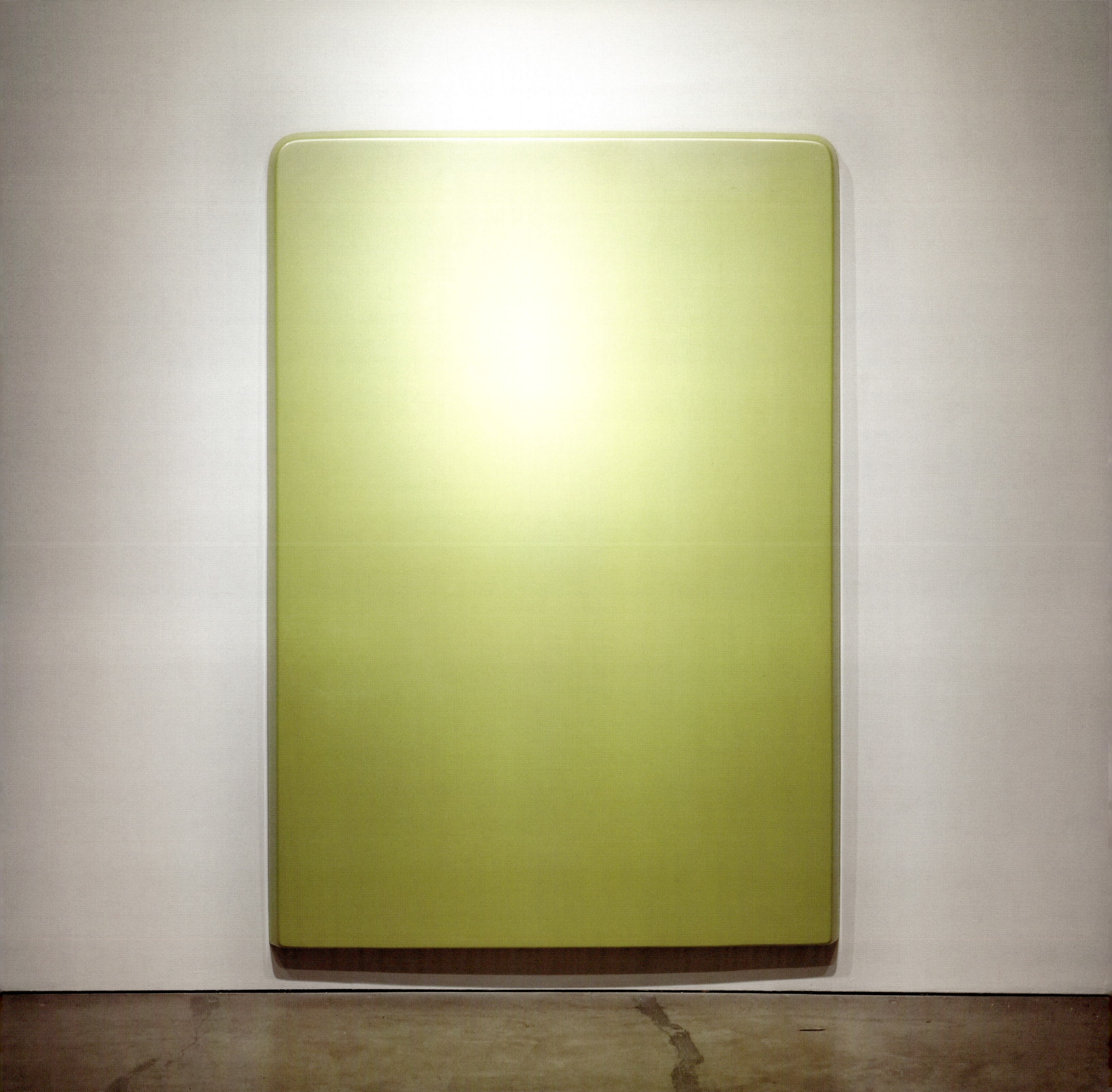

15 *Untitled (iridescent yellow panel)*, 2005, polyurethane on fiberglass, 6' 5" × 5' 6"

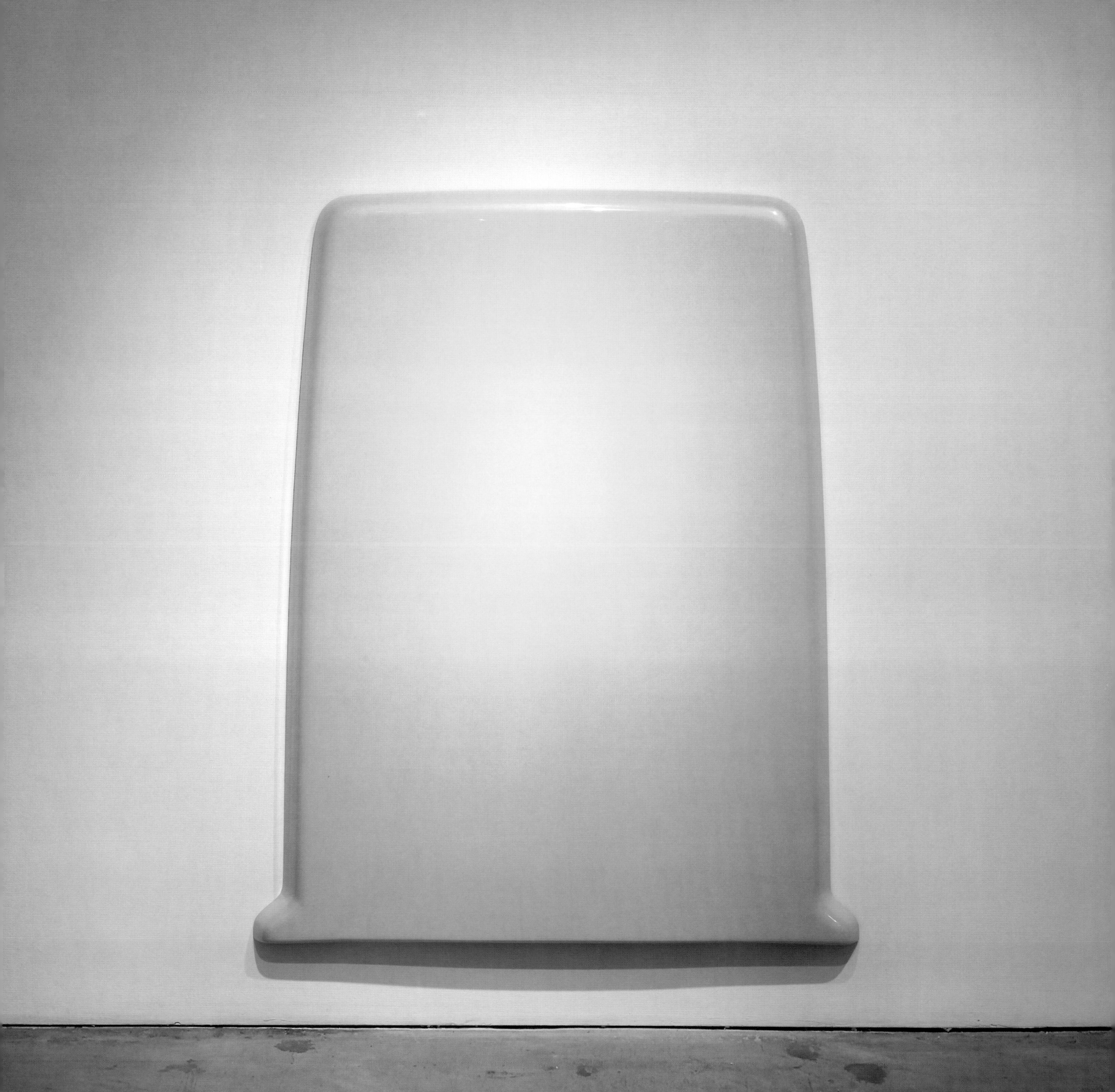

16 *Untitled (iridescent silver panel)*, 2005, polyurethane on fiberglass, 6' 5" × 5' 5"

17 *Untitled (red20)*, 2001, polyurethane on wood, 10' x 8'

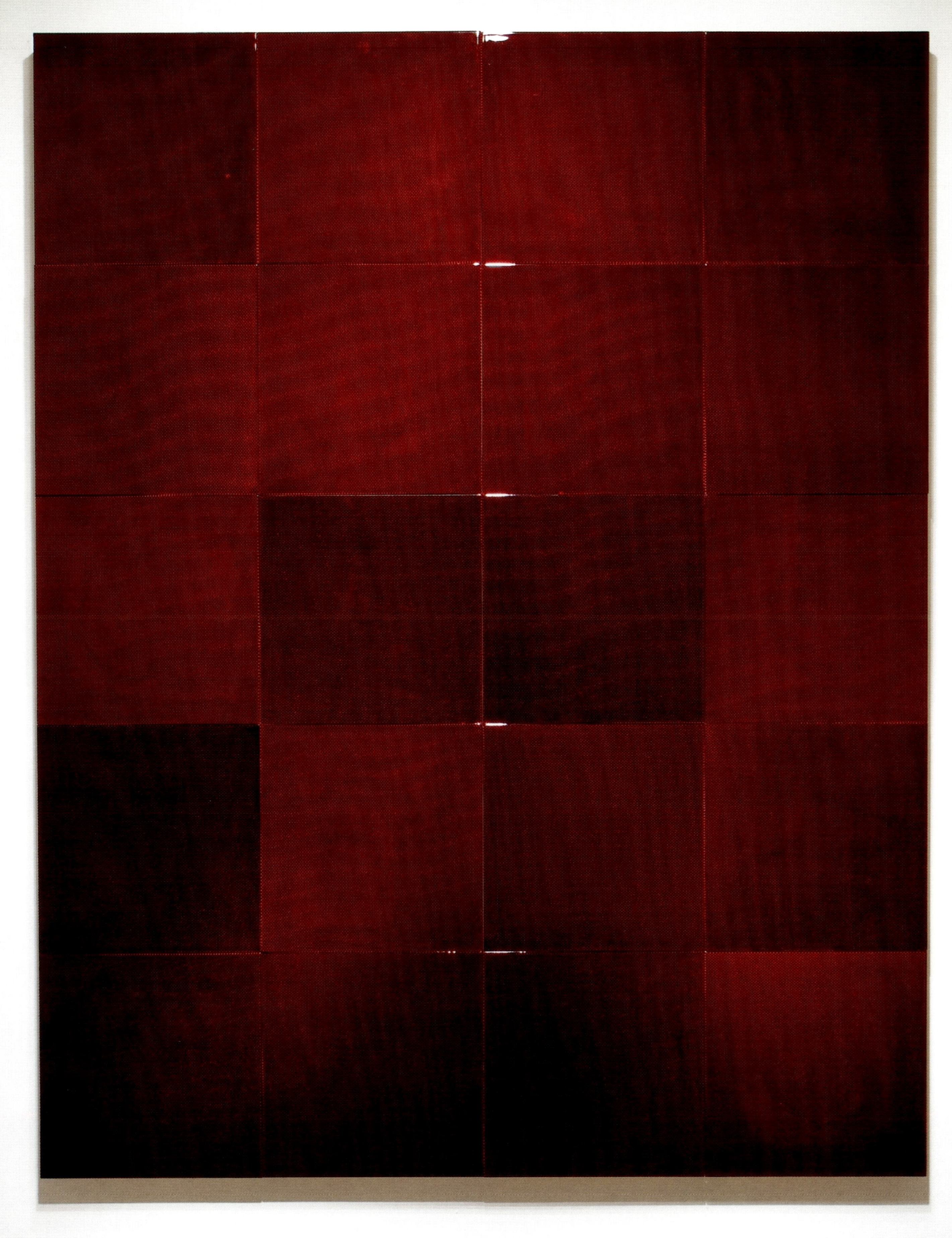

18 *Untitled (iridescent slate15)*, 2004, polyurethane on wood, 9' 3" × 5' 7"

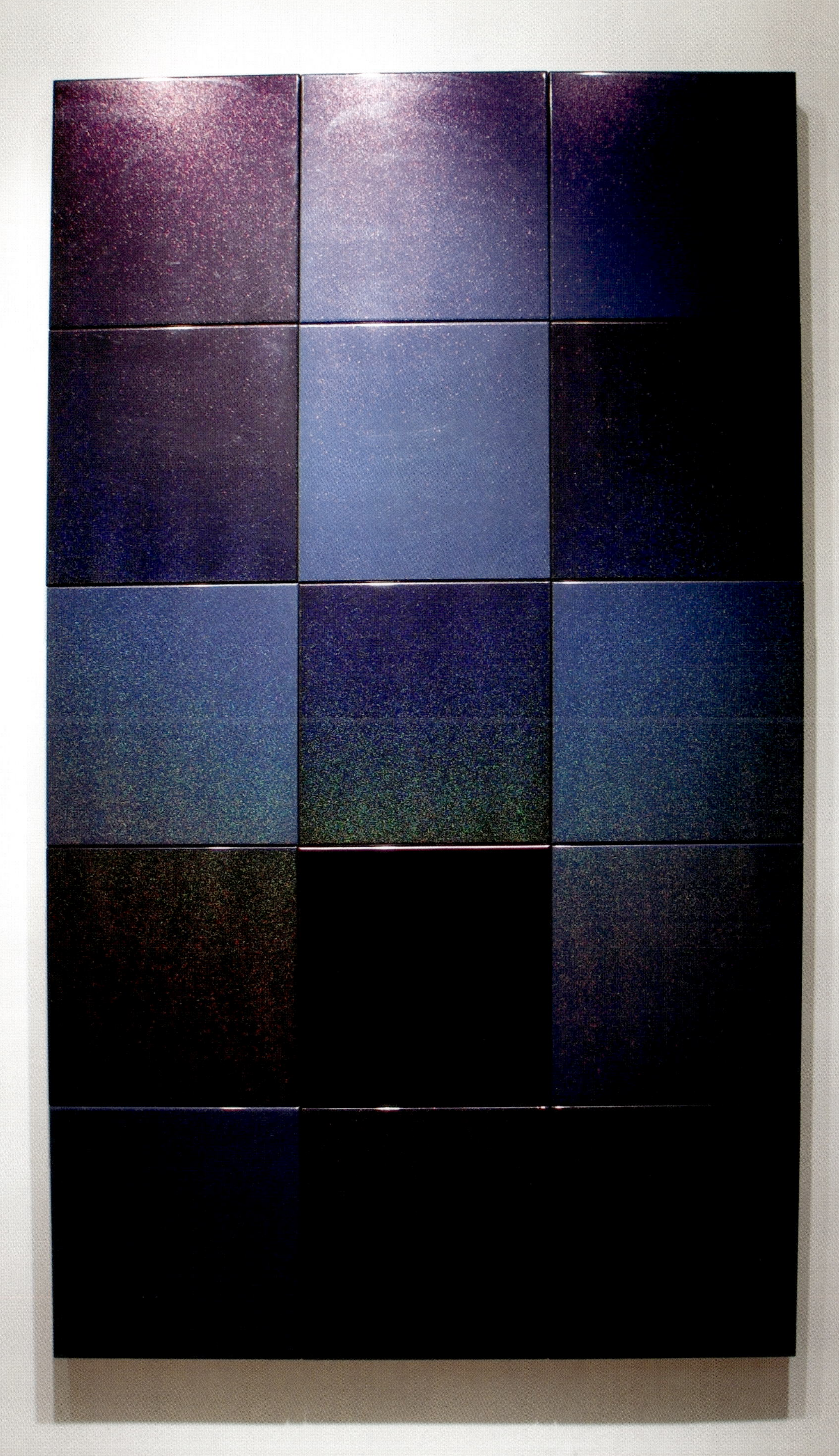

19 *Untitled (red squiggle6)*, 2004, resin epoxy on wood, 9' × 6'

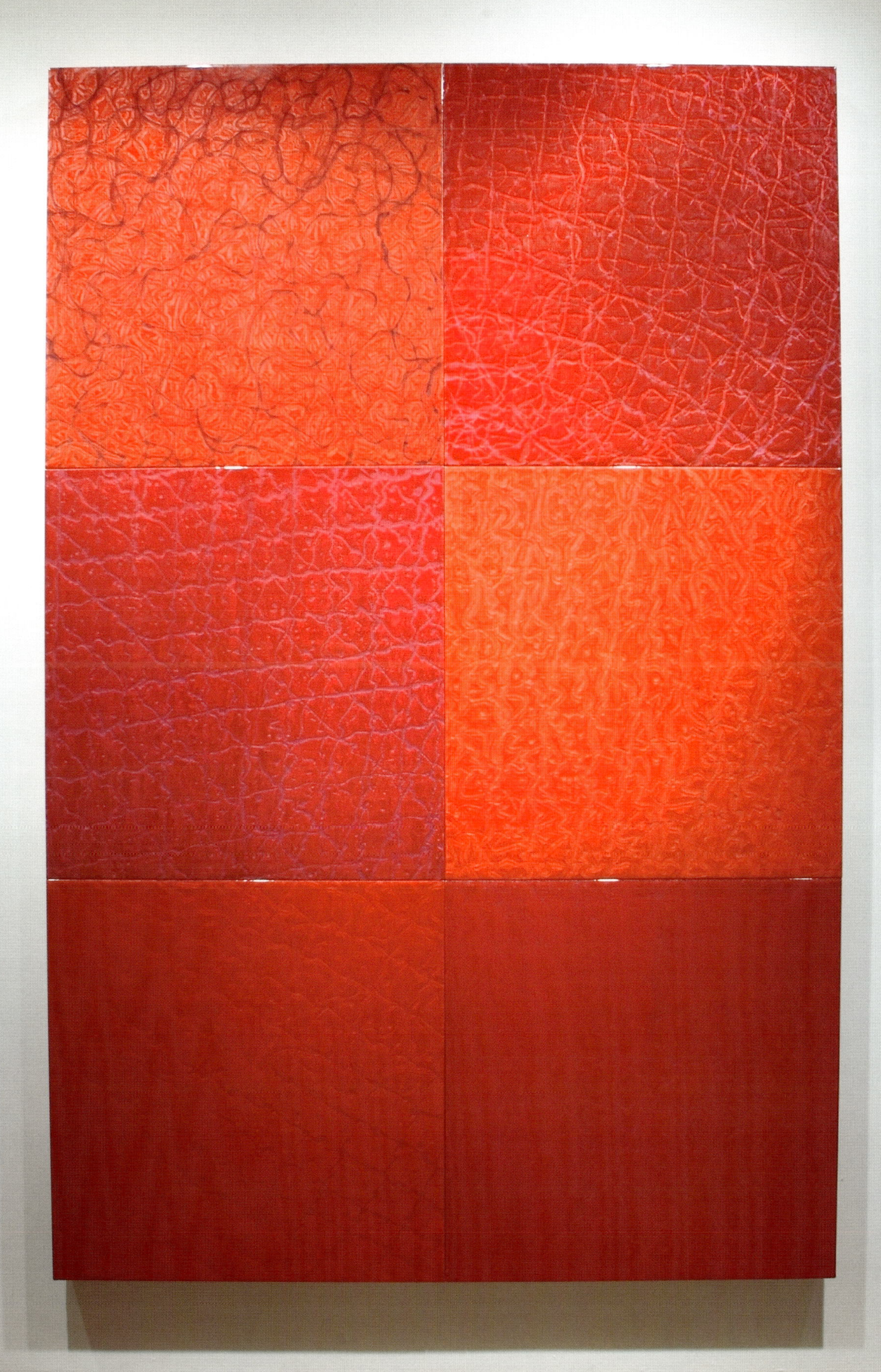

20 *Untitled (magenta16)*, 2003, polyurethane on wood, 12' × 12'

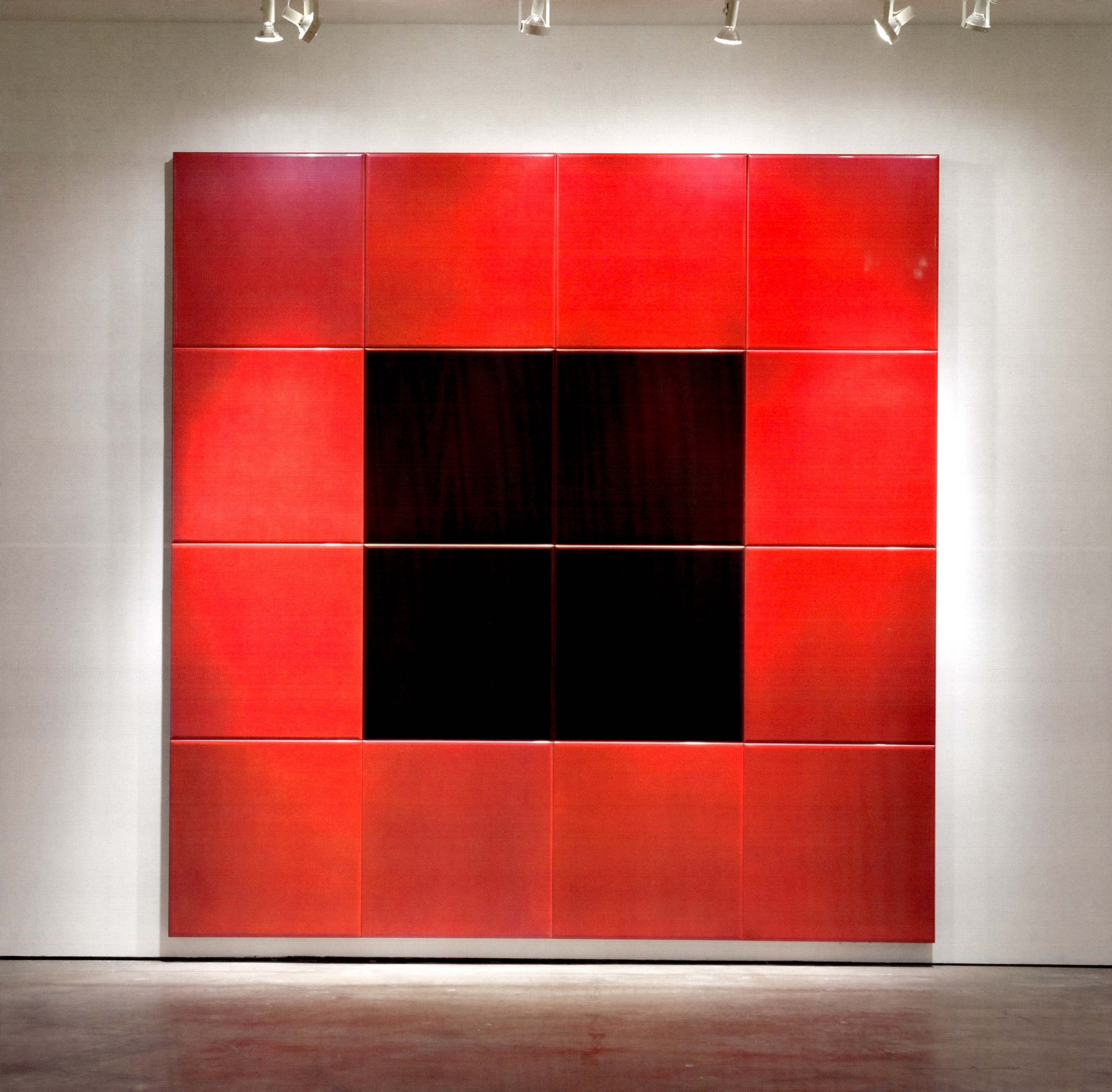

21 *Untitled (black mark/amber/vertical3)*, 1994, resin epoxy on wood, 12' × 12'

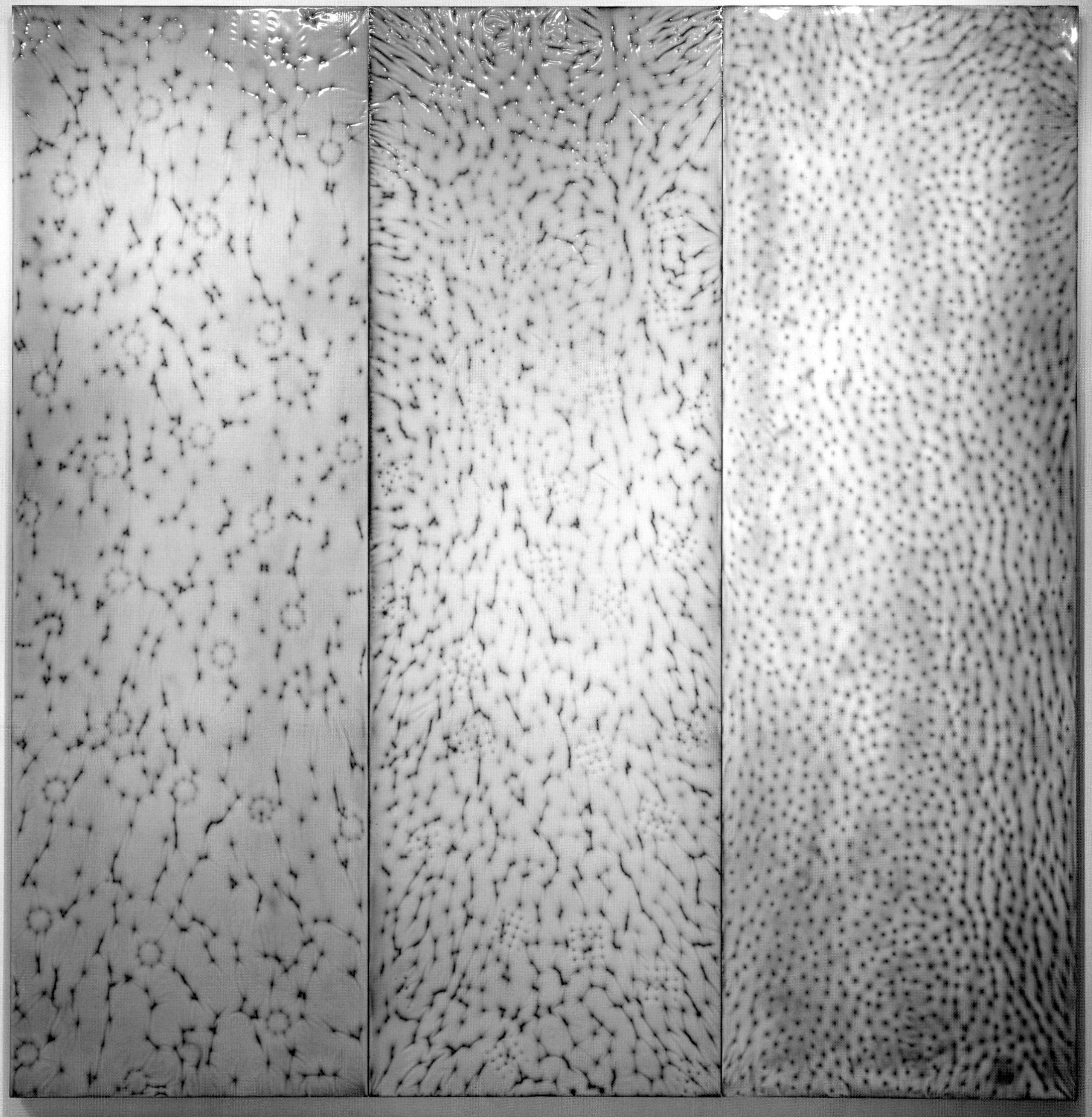

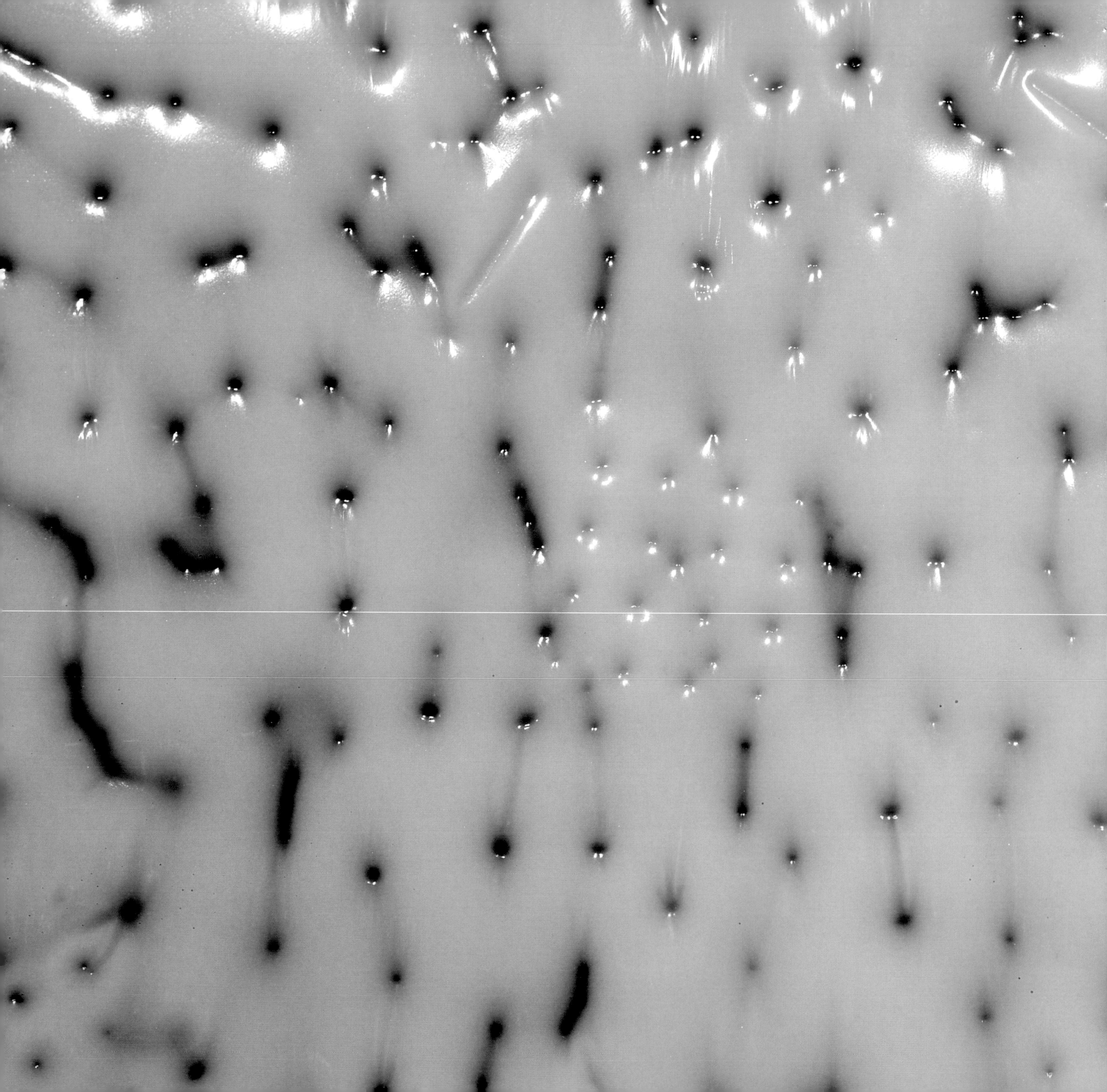

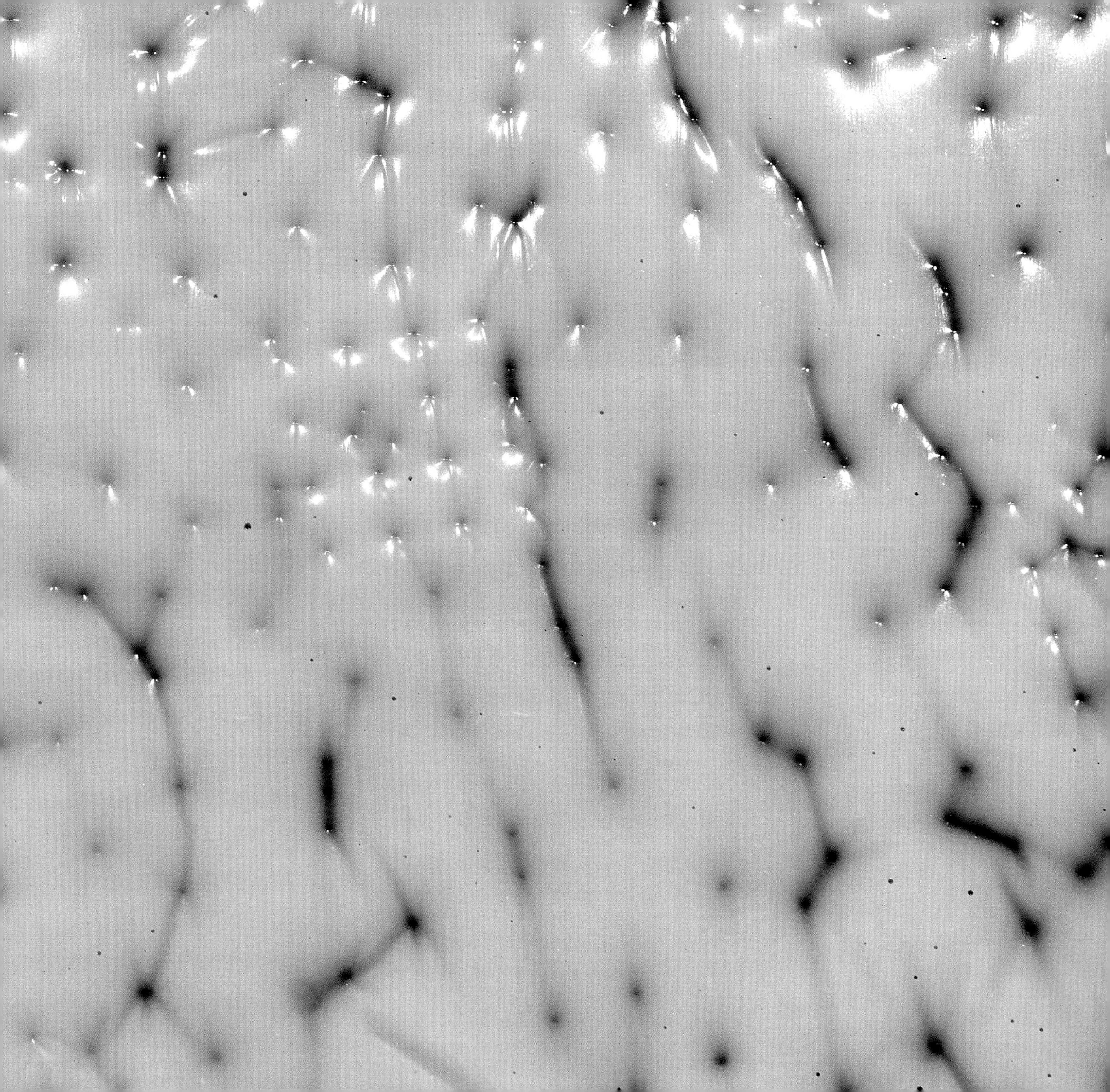

22 *Untitled (white mark/black/vertical3)*, 1994, resin epoxy on wood, 12' × 12'

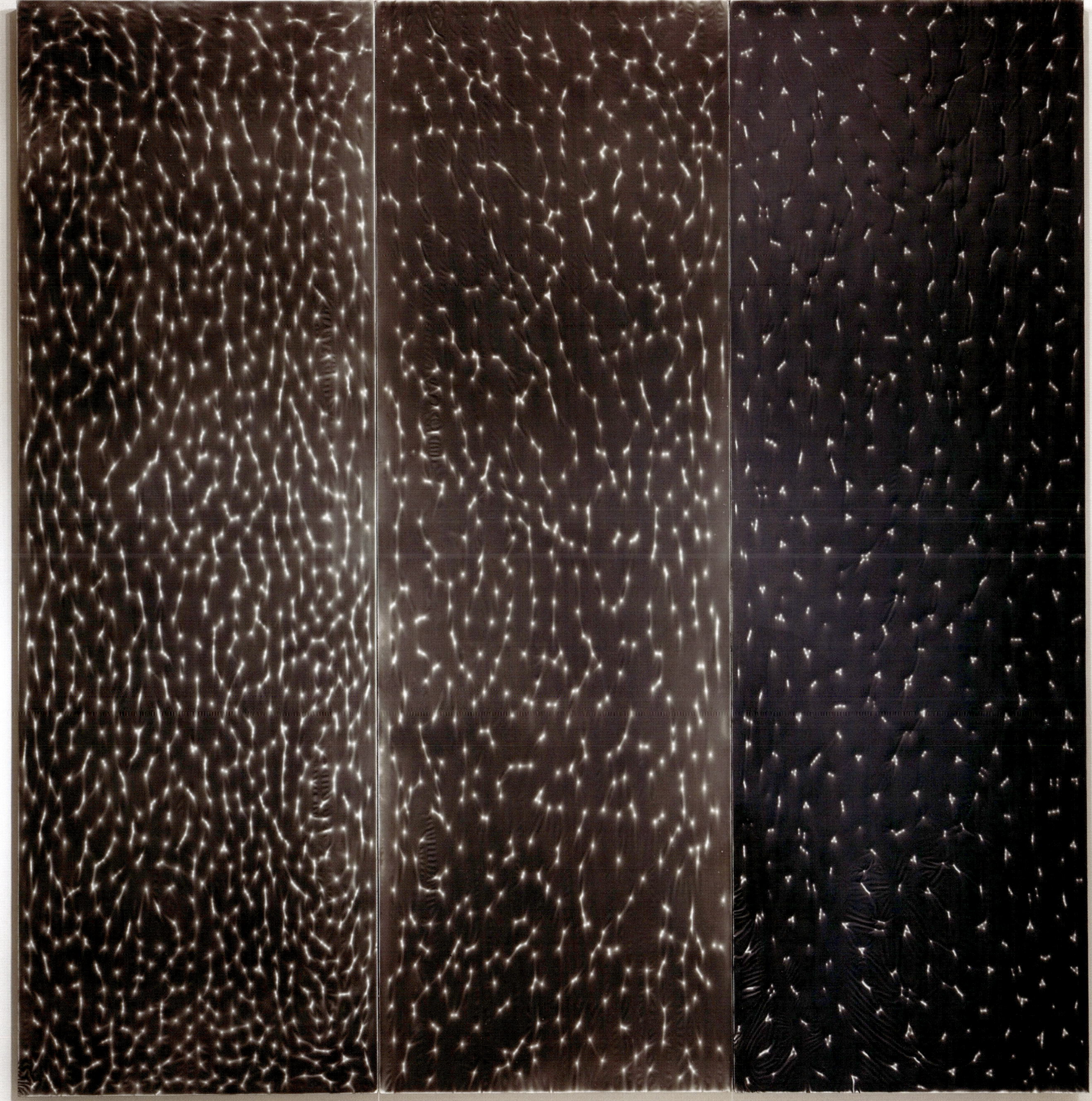

23 | *Untitled (copper dot3)*, 1992, resin epoxy on wood, 12' × 12'

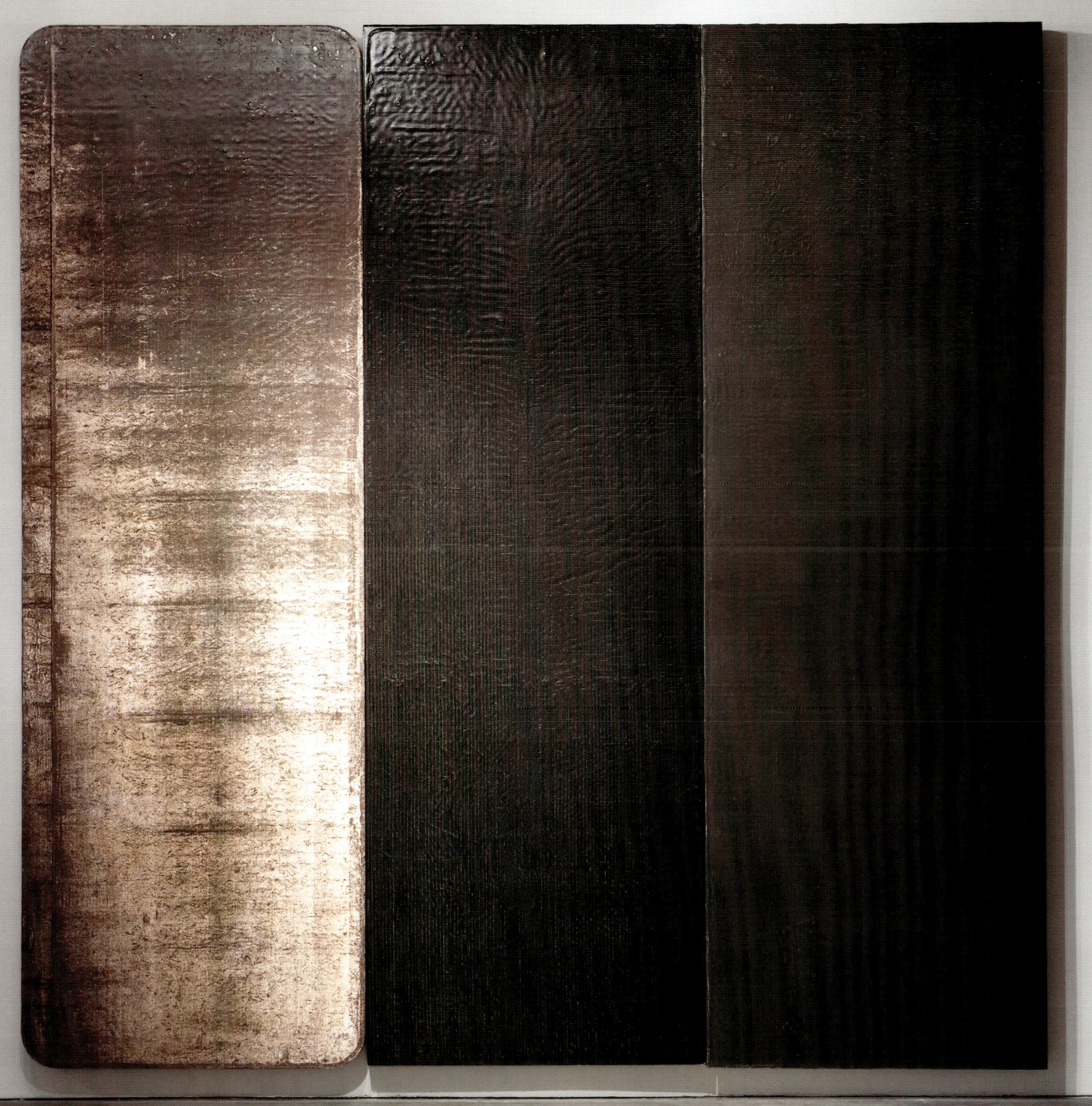

24 | *Untitled (center stripe3)*, 1993, resin epoxy on wood, 12' × 12'

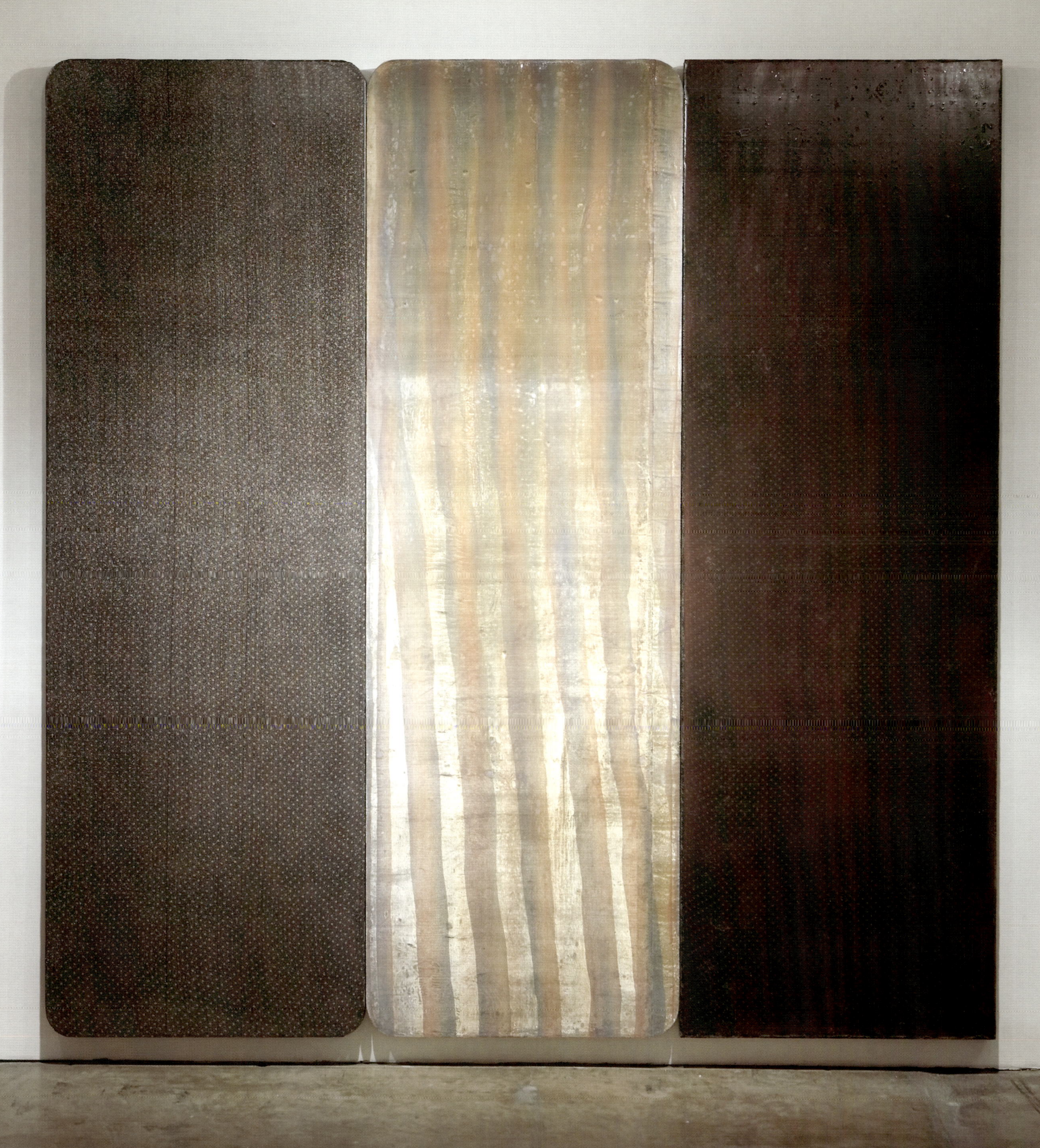

25 *Untitled (multicolor32)*, 2004, polyurethane on wood, 7' 5" × 14' 11"

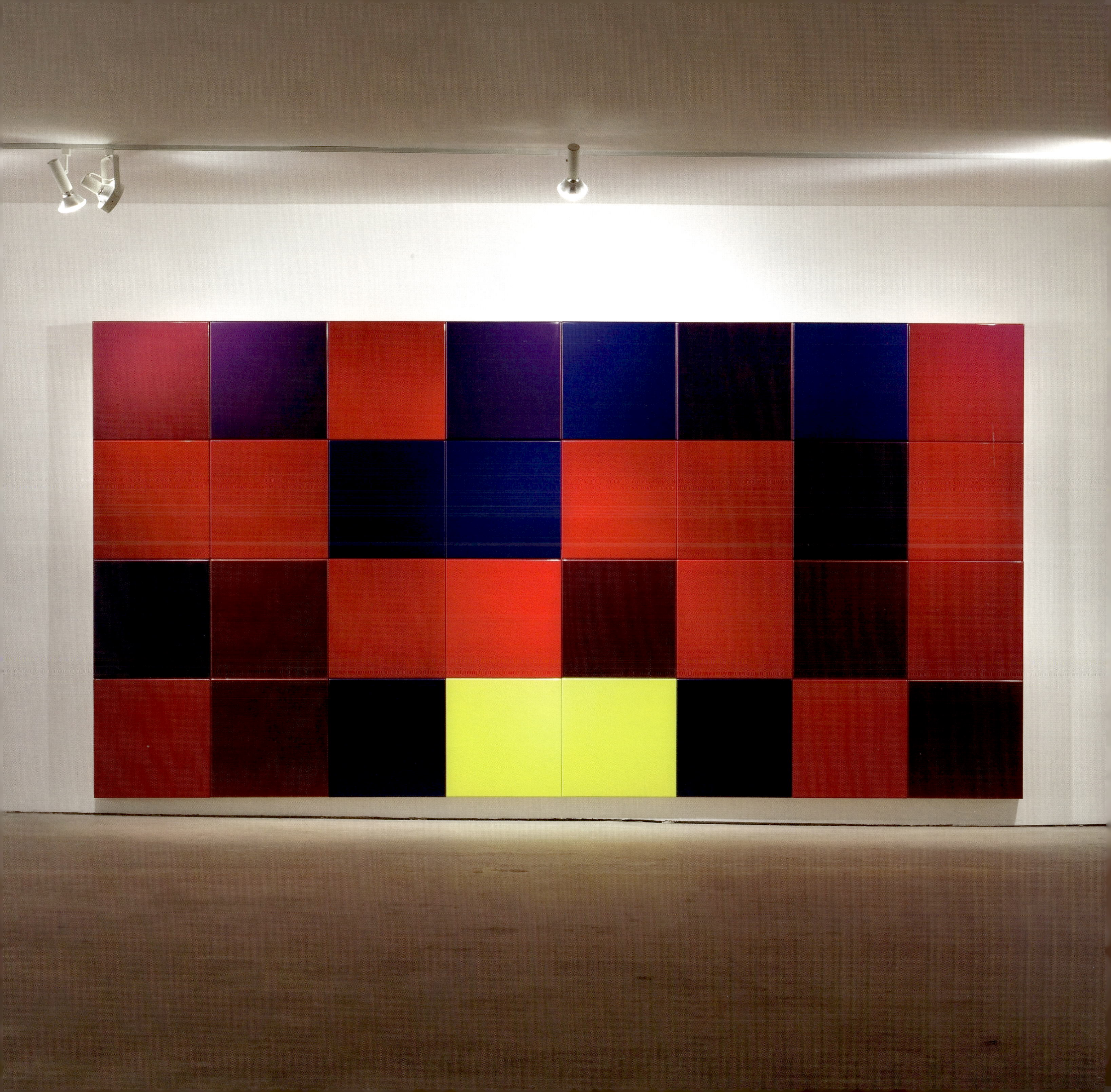

 Untitled (studies), 1998–2004, resin epoxy on wood, dimensions variable

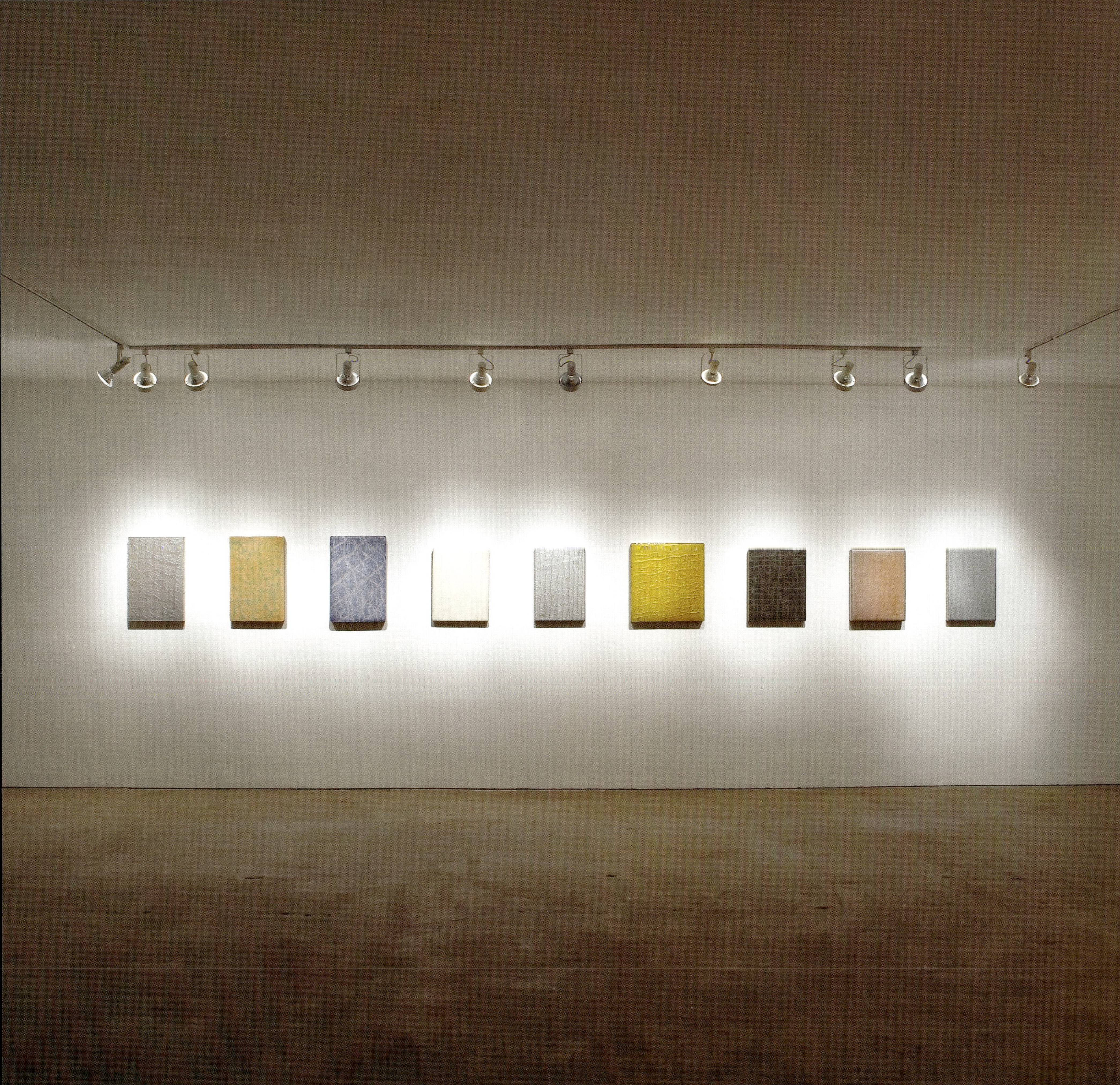

27 *Untitled (studies),* 1998–2004, resin epoxy on wood, dimensions variable

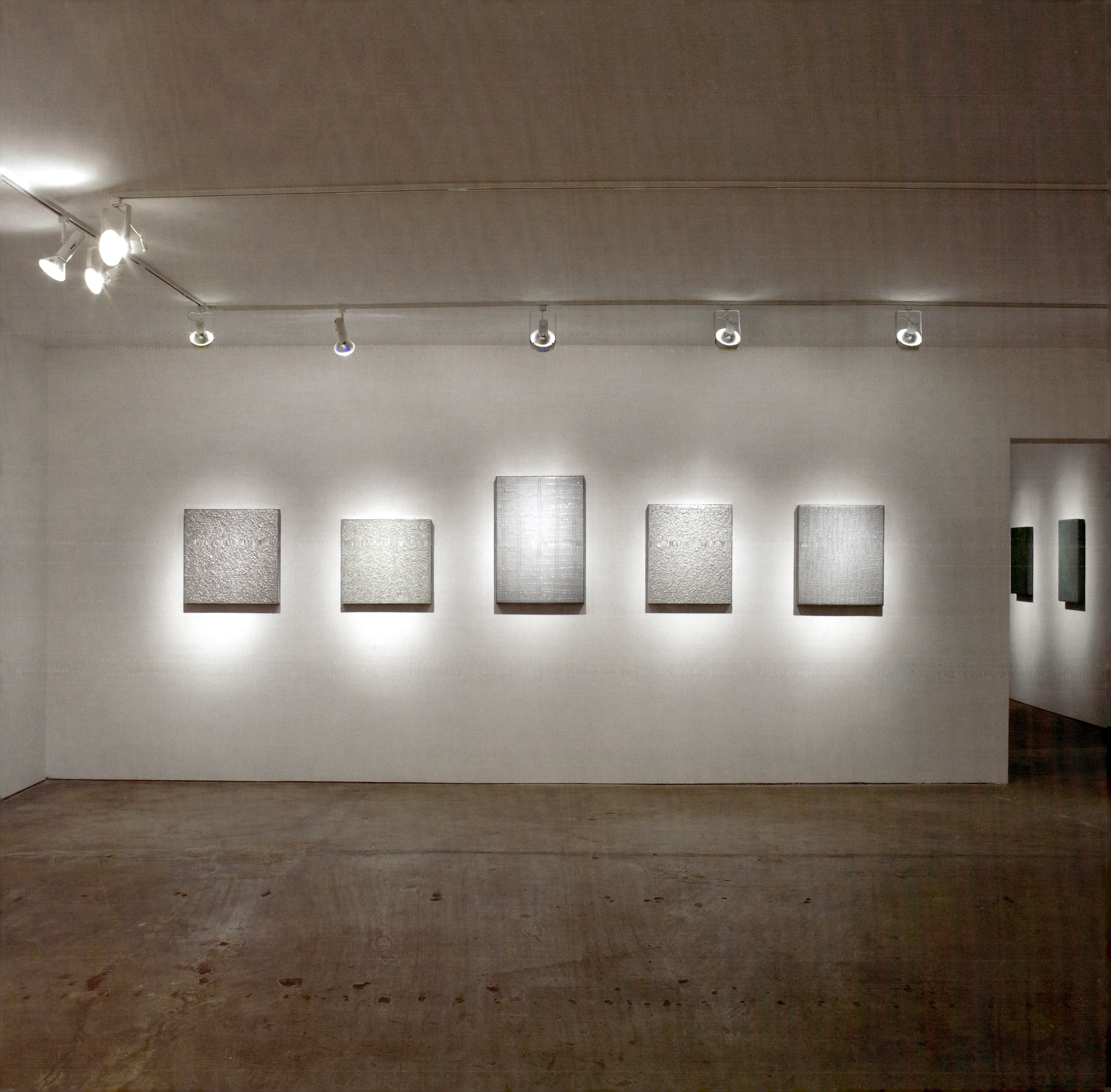

EXHIBITION CHECKLIST

Untitled (El Paso), 1971–72, acrylic on canvas, 14' × 21'

Untitled (copper dot3), 1992, resin epoxy on wood, 12' × 12'

Untitled (center stripe3), 1993, resin epoxy on wood, 12' × 12'

Untitled (black mark/amber/vertical3), 1994, resin epoxy on wood, 12' × 12'

Untitled (white mark/black/vertical3), 1994, resin epoxy on wood, 12' × 12'

Untitled (studies), 1998–2004, series of 18 panels, resin epoxy on wood, dimensions variable

Untitled (blue8, shape2), 1999, resin epoxy on wood, 10' × 25'

Untitled (orange32), 2000, polyurethane on wood, 12' × 24'

Untitled (light blue8), 2001, polyurethane on wood, 12' × 6'

Untitled (red20), 2001, polyurethane on wood, 10' × 8'

Untitled (magenta16), 2003, polyurethane on wood, 12' × 12'

Untitled (multicolor32), 2004, polyurethane on wood, 7' 5" × 14' 11"

Untitled (iridescent slate15), 2004, polyurethane on wood, 9' 3" × 5' 7"

Untitled (red squiggle6), 2004, resin epoxy on wood, 9' × 6'

Untitled (silver45), 2004, polyurethane on wood, 9' 3" × 16' 8"

Untitled (silver16), 2004, polyurethane on wood, 12' × 12'

Untitled (silver27), 2004, polyurethane on wood, 8' 7" × 12'

Untitled (blue/yellow42), 2005, polyurethane on wood, 11' 8" × 6' 5"

Untitled (white line51), 2005, polyurethane on wood, 10' 11" × 12'

Untitled (left leaning yellow51), 2005, polyurethane on wood, 14' × 7' 5"

Untitled (iridescent yellow panel), 2005, polyurethane on fiberglass, 6' 5" × 5' 0"

Untitled (iridescent silver panel), 2005, polyurethane on fiberglass, 6' 5" × 5' 5"

Untitled (light yellow panel), 2005, polyurethane on fiberglass, 6' 9" × 4' 11"

Untitled (right leaning red51), 2005, polyurethane on wood, 14' × 7' 5"

Untitled (bronze/green42), 2005, polyurethane on wood, 6' 5" × 11' 8"

Untitled (red line51), 2005, polyurethane on wood, 10' 11" × 12'

Untitled (multicolor line51), 2005, polyurethane on wood, 12' × 10' 11"

Untitled (concave15), 2005, polyurethane on wood, 8' × 12' 6"

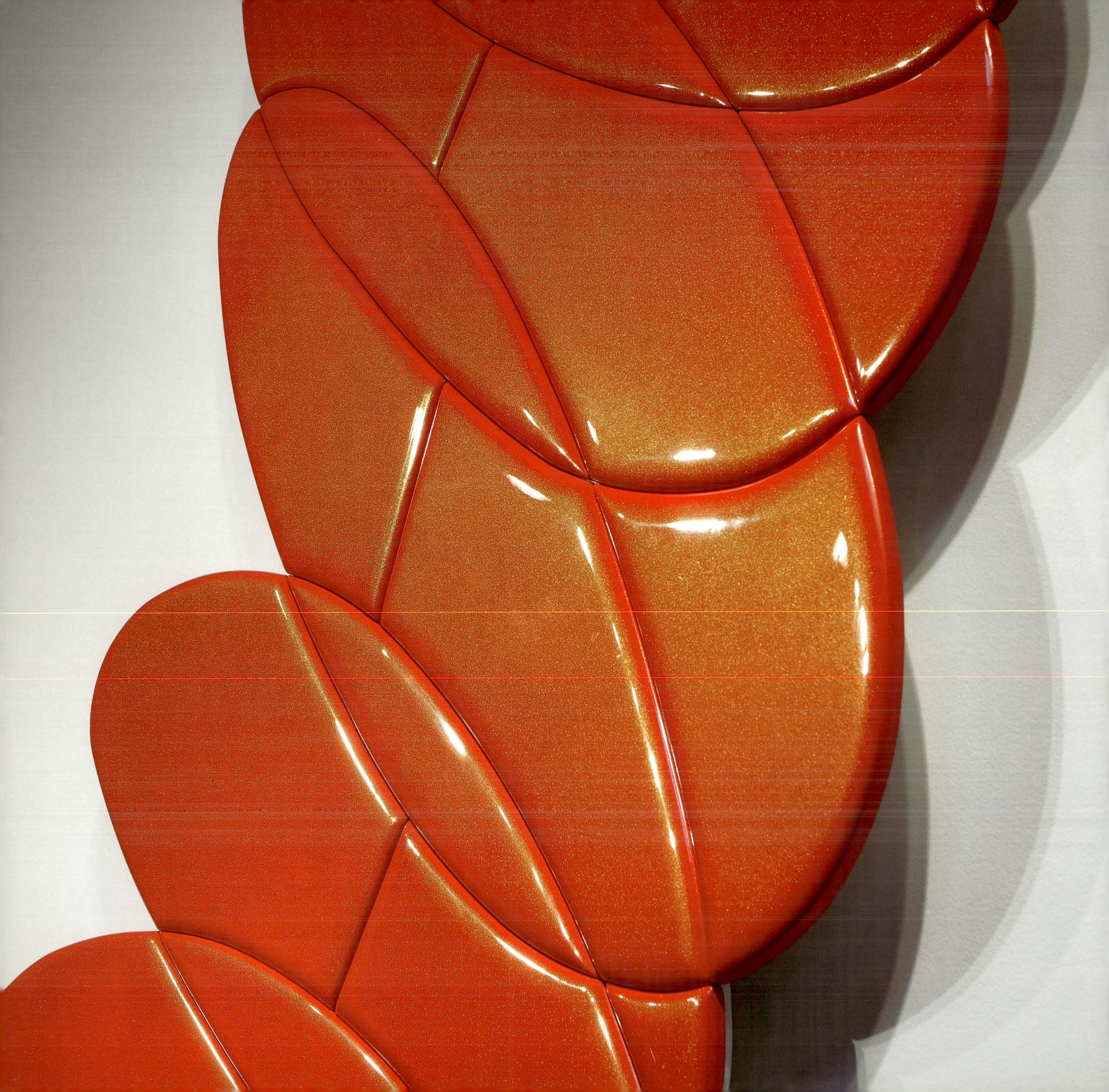

BIOGRAPHY

Born in 1928, Chicago, Illinois.

EDUCATION

1945–48 The School of the Art Institute of Chicago, Illinois

1953–54 Otis Art Institute, Los Angeles, California

1955–56 Mexico City College, Mexico

ONE-PERSON EXHIBITIONS

2005 SITE Santa Fe, New Mexico

1984 Tomasula Gallery, Union County College, Cranford, New Jersey

1982 Nancy Hoffman Gallery, New York, New York

Southwest Artists Series, Aspen Center for Visual Arts, Colorado

University of New Mexico Art Museum, Albuquerque

1981 ARCO Center for the Visual Arts, Los Angeles, California

Fendrick Gallery, Washington, D.C.

1980 Nancy Hoffman Gallery, New York, New York

Wright State University, Dayton, Ohio

Traveled to: Herron Gallery, Indianapolis, Indiana; Ohio State University, Columbus

1979 The Arts Club of Chicago, Illinois

opposite: detail of *Untitled (right leaning red51)*, [plate 7]

1978	Nancy Hoffman Gallery, New York, New York
1977	Museum of Contemporary Arts, Houston, Texas
1975	*Feature Painting*, Museum of Contemporary Arts, Houston, Texas
1973	Michael Walls Gallery, Los Angeles, California
1972	Museum of Contemporary Art, Chicago, Illinois
1970	Santa Barbara Museum of Art, California
	Michael Walls Gallery, San Francisco, California
1969	Corcoran Gallery of Art, Washington, D.C.
1968	Pasadena Art Museum, California
1963	La Jolla Art Center, California
1962	Aura Gallery, Pasadena, California
1958	Nova Gallery, Boston, Massachusetts

SELECTED GROUP EXHIBITIONS

1999	*Radical P.A.S.T.: Contemporary Art & Music in Pasadena, 1960-74*, Armory Center for the Arts, Pasadena, California
	Postmark: An Abstract Effect, SITE Santa Fe, New Mexico
1993	*Trompe L'Oeil Illusionism: Curators' Forum*, Hans and Walter Bechtler Gallery, Charlotte, North Carolina
1992	*The Allure of Illusionism: Trompe L'Oeil in Contemporary American Painting*, Nora Eccles Harrison Museum of Art, Utah State University, Logan
1989	*Alcove Show*, Museum of Fine Arts, Santa Fe, New Mexico
1988	*Directors Invitational*, Helen B. Murray Gallery, Tacoma Art Museum, Washington
1986	*New Mexico Collections*, Fogelson Library, College of Santa Fe, New Mexico

1985 *Abstract Variations*, Harcourts Contemporary, San Francisco, California

The Real Thing: Trompe L'Oeil, Castle Gallery, College of New Rochelle, New York

1984 *American Art Now! Painting in the '80s*, The Columbus Museum, Columbus, Georgia

American Scene, Adams-Middleton Gallery, Dallas, Texas

Still Life Show, Fendrick Gallery, Washington, D.C.

1983 *Salon D'Automne*, Grand Palais, Paris, France

Material Illusions/Unlikely Materials, Taft Museum, Cincinnati, Ohio

1982 *Works on Paper*, Nancy Hoffman Gallery, New York, New York

1981 *45th Annual National Midyear Show*, The Butler Institute of American Art, Youngstown, Ohio

Contemporary Realism, Brainard Art Gallery, S.U.N.Y., College of Arts and Sciences, Potsdam, New York

The Artist and the Airbrush, San Jose State University Art Gallery, California

Still Life/Interiors, Contemporary Arts Center, New Orleans, Louisiana

Contemporary American Realism Since 1960, Pennsylvania Academy of Fine Arts, Philadelphia

Traveled to: Virginia Museum of Fine Art, Richmond; Oakland Museum of Art, California; the Gulbenkian Museum, Lisbon, Portugal; The Salas de Exposiciones de Bellas Artes, Madrid, Spain; and the Kunsthalle Nuremberg, Germany

Real, Really Real and Super Real, San Antonio Museum of Art, Texas

Traveled to: Indianapolis Museum of Art, Indiana; Tucson Museum of Art, Arizona; Museum of Art, Carnegie Institute, Pittsburgh, Pennsylvania

1980 *A Decade of Drawing in Black and White: 1970–80*, The Brooklyn Museum, New York

Realism/Photo Realism, Philbrook Art Center, Tulsa, Oklahoma

Contemporary Naturalism: Works of the '70s, Nassau County Museum of Art, Roslyn, New York

American Art Since 1950, Santa Barbara Museum of Art, California

1979 *The First Western States Biennial Exhibition,* organized by the Western States Arts Foundation, Denver Art Museum, Colorado

Traveled to: San Francisco Museum of Modern Art, California; Seattle Art Museum, Washington; University of Hawaii, Honolulu; Newport Harbor Art Museum, California

Prospectus: The Seventies, The Aldrich Museum of Contemporary Art, Ridgefield, Connecticut

Still Life, Lamont Gallery, Phillips Exeter Academy, Exeter, New Hampshire

Things Seen: The Concept of Realism in 20th–Century Art, Sheldon Memorial Art Gallery, Lincoln, Nebraska

The Reality of Illusion, Denver Art Museum, Colorado

1978 *Drawing the Line*, Montclair Art Museum, New Jersey

Watercolors, Thomas Segal Gallery, Boston, Massachusetts

1977 *Illusions of Reality*, organized by the Australia Council, National Gallery of Australia, Canberra

Traveled to: Western Australian Gallery, Perth

Painting in the Age of Photography, Kunsthaus Zurich, Switzerland

New Realism, Jacksonville Museum of Modern Art, Florida

Painting and Sculpture in California: The Modern Era, National Collection of Fine Arts, Smithsonian Institution, Washington, D.C.

A View of the Decade, Museum of Contemporary Art, Chicago, Illinois

1976 *Painting and Sculpture in California, The Modern Era*, San Francisco Museum of Modern Art, California

Possibilities, Des Moines Art Center, Iowa

Painting and Sculpture Today, 1976, Indianapolis Museum of Art, Indiana

12 Contemporary Artists Working in New Mexico, Museum of Fine Arts, Santa Fe, New Mexico

Drawings, Monique Knowlton Gallery, New York, New York

1975 *34th Corcoran Biennial*, The Corcoran Gallery of Art, Washington, D.C.

1974 *The Peter Ludwig Collection*, Contemporary Art Museum, Zurich, Switzerland

Watercolor Show, Louis K. Meisel Gallery, New York, New York

71st American Exhibition, Art Institute of Chicago, Illinois

1973 *Separate Realities*, Los Angeles Municipal Art Gallery, Barnsdall Park, California

1972 *Documenta V*, Kassel, West Germany

Surrealism is Alive and Well in the West, Baxter Art Gallery, California Institute of Technology, Pasadena

1971 *American Paintings and Prints*, National Gallery of Australia, Canberra

1970 *Excellence: Art from the University Community*, University Art Gallery, Berkeley, California

Looking West, Joslyn Art Museum, Omaha, Nebraska

1969 *Whitney Annual*, Whitney Museum of American Art, New York, New York

1968 *Late Fifties at the Ferus*, Los Angeles County Museum of Art, California

1965 *Art '65 East and West*, American Pavilion, New York World's Fair, Queens, New York

1960 *Annual*, Pasadena Art Museum, California

1957 *Gallery Artists Group Show*, Ferus Gallery, Los Angeles, California

1954 *The Merry-Go-Round Show*, Carousel Building, Santa Monica Pier, California

Southern California Painting and Sculpture Annual, Los Angeles County Museum of Art, California

Group Show, Walter Hopps Syndell Studio, Brentwood, California

1952 *California Painting Annual*, The De Young Museum, San Francisco, California

SELECTED PUBLIC COLLECTIONS

Aachen Museum, West Germany

Albuquerque Museum of Art and History, New Mexico

Arkansas Art Center, Little Rock

Art Institute of Chicago, Illinois

Atlantic Richfield Company, Los Angeles, California

Becton, Dickinson & Company, Paramus, New Jersey

Corcoran Gallery of Art, Washington, D.C.

Des Moines Art Center, Iowa

Des Moines Register and Tribune, Iowa

Georgia Museum of Art, University of Georgia, Athens

Harwood Museum of Art, Taos, New Mexico

Hirshhorn Museum and Sculpture Garden, Washington, D.C.

Hospital Corporation of America Collection, Nashville, Tennessee

Indianapolis Museum of Art, Indiana

Ludwig Collection, Museum of Modern Art, Vienna

Metropolitan Museum of Art, New York, New York

Milwaukee Art Museum, Wisconsin

Minneapolis Institute of Arts, Minnesota

Museum of Fine Arts, Santa Fe, New Mexico

Oakland Museum, California

Pacific Enterprise Corporation, Los Angeles, California

Pasadena Art Museum, California

Philip Morris Inc., New York, New York

Rose Art Museum, Brandeis University, Waltham, Massachusetts

Santa Barbara Museum of Art, California

Sheldon Memorial Art Gallery, Lincoln, Nebraska

University of New Mexico Art Museum, Albuquerque

Vassar College, Poughkeepsie, New York

Frederick R. Weisman Art Museum, Minneapolis, Minnesota

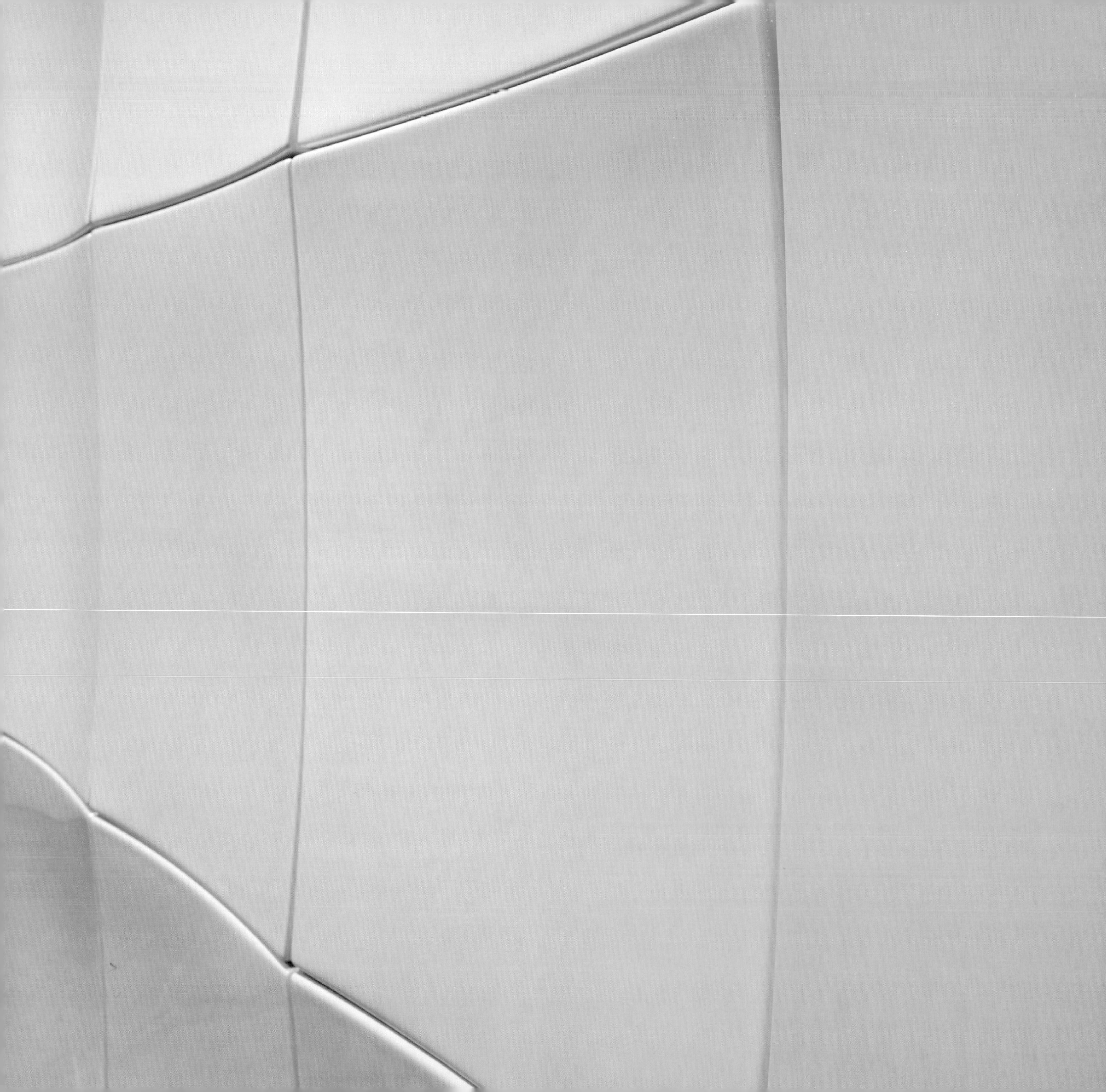

ACKNOWLEDGMENTS

There have been many people involved with this exhibition for the past several years to whom I would like to express my gratitude. Let me begin by thanking Louis Grachos, former director of SITE Santa Fe and current director of the Albright-Knox Art Gallery, Buffalo, New York. Since the inception of this exhibition, his curatorial insight and guidance have remained focused on the tasks at hand and have been invaluable in its realization. In addition, this exhibition would not have been possible without the contributions of Carol Sarkisian, Peter Sarkisian and Lisa Wynne, Christopher Cordes, David Chickey, Sam Brayshaw, Clarence Pacheco, Cathy Weber, Joe Martinez, Michael Moran, Dick and Dottie Barrett, Craig Anderson, Mike Arnold, John Oliver, Bob Richardson, Emmett Flowers, and Megan Prater.

Finally, I wholeheartedly acknowledge the entire staff of SITE Santa Fe for their planning and hard work, which have been essential in making this exhibition a reality, as well as extending thanks to my friends who have given me encouragement and support.

—PAUL SARKISIAN

This exhibition would not have been possible without the hard work of many dedicated and talented people. First, I would like to express my gratitude to Paul Sarkisian as well as Carol and Peter Sarkisian for their major contributions to the exhibition and catalogue. In addition, I would like to thank the entire Board of Directors of SITE Santa Fe, especially Bobbie Foshay-Miller and Marlene Meyerson. I gratefully acknowledge the invaluable efforts of Catherine Putnam, Joanne Lefrak, and Anne Wrinkle. The catalogue would not have been possible without the editing, writing, and advisement of Sarah S. King as well as the design by David Chickey and writing of Christopher Cordes. I would also like to thank Charles A. Stainback for keeping this exhibition on course. Last but definitely not least, I would like to recognize the incredible efforts of Tyler Auwarter and his installation crew, including David Benner, Reanna Cool, Lisa Corradino, Brett Ellison, Pam Ellison, Steven Fowler, Robert Hernandez, Franky Kong, David Marshall, Clayton Porter, Peter Sprunt, and Colin Zaug.

—LOUIS GRACHOS

opposite: detail of *Untitled (concave15)*, [plate 9]

SITE Santa Fe would like to acknowledge the following institutions and individuals for their charitable support of the exhibition:

The Burnett Foundation

The Brown Foundation, Inc., of Houston

The Ford Foundation—New Directions/New Donors for the Arts Initiative

New Mexico Arts, a division of the Department of Cultural Affairs, and the National Endowment for the Arts

The City of Santa Fe Arts Commission and the 1% Lodgers' Tax

The Stockman Family Foundation

Thaw Charitable Trust

Dottie & Dick Barrett

Pat T. Hall

Barbara & Michael Ogg

Joann & Gifford Phillips

SITE Santa Fe is grateful to its Board of Directors and Foundation Council for their ongoing leadership and generous support.

This catalogue has been published on the occasion of the exhibition: PAUL SARKISIAN
May 28–August 28, 2005

SITE Santa Fe
1606 Paseo de Peralta, Santa Fe, New Mexico 87501
Tel: 505.989.1199 Fax: 505.989.1188
www.sitesantafe.org

ISBN: 09764492-2-6
Library of Congress Control Number: 2005926619

Photography: Eric Swanson
Cover: Herb Lotz

Design: David Chickey, Skolkin + Chickey, Santa Fe

Editor: Sarah S. King
Managing Editor: Joanne Lefrak
Associate Editors: Diane Armitage, Katia Zavistovski
Printed in China

All installation views reproduced in this publication were photographed at SITE Santa Fe, 2005.